746.44　　　　　　　　　　　　161961
Loc

Lockwood.
Art embroidery.

Learning Resources Center
Nazareth College of Rochester, N. Y.

THE ÆSTHETIC MOVEMENT & THE ARTS AND CRAFTS MOVEMENT.

EDITED BY PETER STANSKY AND RODNEY SHEWAN. FORTY-EIGHT OF THE MOST IMPORTANT BOOKS, REPRINTED IN THIRTY-EIGHT VOLUMES. GARLAND PUBLISHING, INC.

ART EMBROIDERY

M. S. LOCKWOOD AND GLAISTER

GARLAND PUBLISHING, INC.
NEW YORK & LONDON
1978

Bibliographical note:

this facsimile has been made
from a copy in the
Metropolitan Museum of Art Library
(156.11/L81)

Library of Congress Cataloging in Publication Data

Lockwood, Mary Smith, 1831-1922.
    Art embroidery.

    (The Aesthetic movement & the arts and crafts movement ; 13)
    Reprint of the 1878 ed. published by M. Ward, London.
    1. Needlework. I. Glaister, Elizabeth, joint author.
II. Title. III. Series.
TT750.L6 1978   746.4'4   76-17758
ISBN 0-8240-2462-1

PRINTED IN THE UNITED STATES OF AMERICA

ART EMBROIDERY

ART EMBROIDERY

A Treatise on the Revived Practice

OF

DECORATIVE NEEDLEWORK

BY

M. S. LOCKWOOD AND E. GLAISTER

*WITH NINETEEN PLATES PRINTED IN COLOURS
FROM DESIGNS BY THOMAS CRANE*

𝕷ondon:
MARCUS WARD & CO., 67 AND 68, CHANDOS STREET, STRAND
AND ROYAL ULSTER WORKS, BELFAST
1878

PUBLISHER'S NOTE.

The title of this work, as it appears on the headings of the pages, differs from the Title-page, owing to the claim of another publishing house to priority in the title "Art Needlework." This was not discovered until it was too late to make the necessary alterations.

CONTENTS.

CHAP.	PAGE
I.—Introductory,	7
II.—On Design,	15
III.—On Colour,	25
IV.—On Materials and Stitches,	35
V.—On Methods and Uses,	47
VI.—On Church Embroidery,	55
VII.—On some kinds of Lace,	61
VIII.—On the Study of Old Needlework,	69
IX.—The Plates,	79

ART NEEDLEWORK.

CHAPTER I.

INTRODUCTORY.

NOT the least important result of the present revival of decorative art is that needlework, so long neglected, is once more practised as an art, properly so called. It is many years since the samplers of our grandmothers gave place to the "fancy-work" of modern times, and we are only now beginning to perceive all the uselessness and ugliness of those productions which have brought this term into such disrepute, and have caused the adoption of one of greater refinement, and at the same time of greater pretension, viz., "Art Needlework."

In order that we may be justified in the use of such a term, we should be fully aware of all that is implied in it, and, not satisfied with merely following a passing fashion, possess ourselves of lasting principles by which to regulate our work—principles that at the same time may be a growing source of refined pleasure, as leading to the cultivation of the artistic sense.

If, therefore, needlework is to be raised to the rank of an art, it must be submitted to the laws and restrictions by which all art is governed—such, for instance, as rule the higher art of painting, with which, though confined within narrower limits, it is closely connected.

The first condition of an ideal work of art is that it should be conceived and carried out by one person; division of labour is fatal to distinction and individuality—it is good for pins, but bad for works of art. From this we see the first defect of the Berlin-wool fancy-work; the pattern being drawn by one person, the colours, &c., selected by a second, the pattern worked by a third, and very often "grounded" by a fourth; whereas in art needlework, that is really worthy of the name, the materials should be chosen, the dimensions fixed, the pattern designed, and the work executed by one and the same person.

It will be seen at once that to do this the workwoman must have special qualifications; but as these qualifications are, after all, neither many nor formidable, and quite within the reach of every cultivated person, this work aspires to enumerate, and, as far as possible, to impart them. At the same time, it may be objected that not every one possesses the necessary power of drawing, and that the acquirement of that power is a slow process; but this is no reason against attempting to represent the simpler forms of nature in accordance with certain rules; and it will be found that, after the first success, progress is rapid. In the meantime, the plates which form part of this work, being designed to show the various modes of employing natural forms in decoration, may be used as guides or hints by the skilled worker, as well as useful practice for the beginner, who, having as yet everything to learn from experience, should follow them more closely.

It is true that in modern times, oftener than formerly, it is possible to procure a fine design drawn by a master, or perhaps a good adaptation of an ancient pattern, which it would seem a more rewarding occupation to reproduce than to spend time in designing for ourselves what might be but of moderate merit; and in such cases there would be so much left to the judgment and taste of the worker as to justify her in calling the result of her labours an Art.

The earlier workwomen—those who produced the first embroidered quilt or hanging—had plainly no one to design for them, and no one to furnish them with any prescribed materials as in the present day; their taste, unhampered by fashion, was original and pure; they followed, unconsciously, those laws which we are now painfully searching out and trying to formulate.

The desire for ornament arose in the earliest times, from the moment that man found himself provided with the necessaries of life; and the first makers of weapons, furniture, and stuffs, while adding decoration to please the eye, took care that it should not interfere with use, or disagree with the nature of the material. They carried out unconsciously the maxim, "Nothing can be ornamental that is not also really useful." Flat surfaces were made interesting and pleasing by patterns that neither by their weight, colour, nor projection were a hindrance to usefulness; objects were in material and construction exactly as they appeared to be, nor did they suggest any use other than was really intended. Thus they ministered to the simple pleasure of the unspoilt eye in harmonious colours and well-arranged lines, instead of gratifying the lower curiosity, the love of surprise, display, and deception characteristic of later times.

Then came a period of sophistication and debasement in ornament, when motives and intentions were confused and exaggerated, and a superficial acquaintance with a number of styles and periods led to a mixture of all, and, in the special department of needlework, produced the "fancy-work" which we all abuse. The reasons of its worthlessness were chiefly a thirst for novelty and a taste for display; the desire of the seller to create a demand for costly materials, and the desire of the buyer to produce the most gay and striking effect with the least possible expenditure of thought, time, or trouble. Thus a debased fancy has run riot among every kind and style of ornament, good and bad, and mingled them with every kind of exaggeration and confusion. The result has been such as we know.

To see all this clearly is one step towards accomplishing better things, and, though we cannot revive the spontaneous simplicity and freedom of the earlier work, we may, by using our finer perceptions and knowledge, produce admirable and beautiful art, so as to adorn our dwellings in a manner worthy of them and ourselves.

Enough has been said to suggest the ideas which should govern the planning and carrying-out of a piece of needlework, and it only remains to state clearly and in their proper order the principles most necessary to be borne in mind.

I.—*Needlework should express intelligence, and give evidence of the direct application of the mind to the material.* In this lies the superiority of hand-work over loom-work. The latter has, for obvious reasons, superseded the former in every case where large quantities are needed and large spaces have to be covered or filled; and, indeed, if the pattern be good and the colouring harmonious, for these purposes it leaves nothing to be desired. But machine-made work has of late been wrongly applied in the production of borders or bands of design intended to look like hand embroidery, and in these its inferiority for such a use is apparent in the monotony and tameness of its appearance

—the very smoothness and perfection of its texture being an additional defect. An intelligent workwoman, especially if she be a designer as well, will feel that perfection of workmanship is by no means to be considered as the most valuable quality of her work; in fact, that this very perfection has, in much of modern production, been attained at the expense of almost everything else that is desirable, and often betrays a desire to show off dexterity and ingenuity—the surest road to vulgarity and bad taste. We should desire our needlework to appeal, like the higher arts, to the finer perceptions; and to cultivate it as an art must necessarily help to develope powers of different kinds—a sense of harmony, fitness, and symmetry, to say nothing of gifts for colour and form that might never have come to light if not employed in this way. The high culture of the present day will not do away with the need which so many feel for the soothing influence of needlework, but to employ in it a better intelligence will be to enhance its value in every way. We can no longer be satisfied with filling up little squares or diamonds ready traced in certain fixed colours on canvas specially prepared, so that nothing may go wrong with the stitches.

II.—*Needlework should be in every way adapted to the materials used.* As the sculptor's chisel and the painter's brush have each their separate function and domain, so has the needle of the embroideress; nor should anything lying beyond its proper powers be attempted by its means. Flowers and foliage being the decorative part of nature, we instinctively choose them for reproduction in needlework. The grand productions of ancient tapestry, containing whole histories of wars and sieges, are never likely to be repeated in our days, in which leisure and industry are both lacking, and we must content ourselves, at least for the moment, with speaking of the lighter works which lie within the ordinary compass of time and patience.

With regard, then, to the imitation of flowers in needlework, it is evident that the imitation must be incomplete, and that less must be attempted than in painting. It is as impossible to reproduce the odour of flowers as it is to imitate the bloom of their texture, the delicacy and evanescence of their more brilliant tints, or the minute details of their form. The attempt must, once for all, be abandoned, and only those aspects of form and colour be chosen which are capable of being adapted and combined so as to produce a satisfactory result in the manner called *conventional*. This limitation is imposed on our art by the nature of its materials, and follows from a just appreciation of what may be successfully accomplished with those materials.

The gaudy obtrusiveness of the Berlin-wool flower-groups is owing to a mistaken apprehension of this very thing, and a desire to imitate natural appearances which are not capable of imitation. Such attempts are at best but coarse and clumsy, and their greatest success is gained when, by means of laborious shading, the flowers appear to stand out from the canvas, so that the cushion or stool seems intended for anything rather than resting a weary head or foot. Ours must be a very different choice. "Realisation to the mind does not necessitate deception to the eye." We must not expect, nor seem to wish others to expect, what is at variance with the nature of things. If we decorate a flat surface, let us be satisfied that the surface should still seem flat; and as curtains, cushions, chair-covers, are intended to be touched or handled, it is false taste and art to try to make them resemble water-colour paintings. To produce an appearance of projection when the surface is flat, or of roughness when it is in reality smooth, is to make one sense contradict another—a poor sort of deception, which involves a great deal of wasted time and ingenuity.

III.—*Needlework should satisfy requirements both of use and beauty.* We must start with the idea of beautifying what is already useful, and rather convey a new sense of repose and ease in the decorative furniture of our rooms than deprive them of their expression of use and comfort. The work should be executed so as to be lasting; it must be of good and genuine materials, well and solidly worked, and have at the same time an appearance of ease in the working. Work that shows great elaboration of design and laboriousness of execution, is seldom beautiful in proportion to the pains expended upon it. Slight irregularities of form and inequalities of stitch often lend a beauty to work, but they are generally happiest when unpremeditated. The larger the surface to be covered with embroidery, the more evenly the colour and pattern should be distributed, so as to enrich the general effect without disturbing the eye. In a piece of work, for whatever use it may be destined, delicacy, simplicity, and repose should be the qualities at which the worker aims, in opposition to extravagance, garishness, and exaggeration.

"Good art is inseparable from delicacy, as bad art is from coarseness." A piece of needlework was lately shown to one of the writers by an aged lady, in whose youth it was not new. It is a piece of cambric, covered with a delicate design of branching flowers and leaves, in gold-coloured silk. It has been washed, worn, and mended till hardly four inches remain without a darn; yet the fragment is still beautiful and interesting. The cambric is genuine and well woven, the silk well dyed and of the best quality—so that its gloss and colour are just what they were nearly a hundred years ago—and the design being exactly suited to the materials, the result still shows the refined and just perceptions of the worker and of the age in which she lived.

It is with a view to the production of such work as this that these hints are intended—work which, to recapitulate, must (1) *express intelligence,* (2) *be adapted to the materials used, and* (3) *satisfy the requirements both of use and beauty.*

CHAPTER II.

ON DESIGN.

E have seen that, the art of needlework being confined within narrower limits than that of painting, it becomes necessary, while adopting natural forms, to conventionalise them to suit our purpose; and that a knowledge of what can and what cannot be accomplished by the means at our command, is the foundation of the art, and also one of the best fruits of our experience.

Roughly speaking, there are two modes of treating natural forms in embroidery. That most suitable for beginners, and most easily adapted to small pieces of work, is what may be termed the natural treatment, where conventionalism is carried no further than is rendered necessary by the nature of the materials and the size and shape of the space to be filled. The other treatment is of a more severe kind; in it certain natural forms are taken as a basis, and from them a design of a more or less formal character is worked out. In this style beautiful patterns may be made, and it is very effective where a certain defined space has to be filled; but a large knowledge and practice of the principles of design are required in order to attain any degree of success; the lines and curves must be guided by a clear idea of what is to be done, they should be free and strong; no weak or loose lines can be allowed; each part must be determined by its relation to the whole, and a perfect balance of all be preserved. This branch of design can best be learned by studying good examples, such as Raphael's Arabesques in the Vatican (of which there are copies in the South Kensington Museum), and other fifteenth and sixteenth century work.

It is beyond the scope of this little work to teach the art of designing; our desire is to give the amateur some help in the first mentioned simpler process, by which the lovely forms of natural objects may be reduced to a simplicity suitable for embroidery, leaving arabesque, cinque-cento, and geometrical design to more experienced hands.

The most severe conventional treatment is that which reduces the design to a mere symbol for the flower intended, as in the heraldic rose and fleur-de-lys, which, in their traditional forms, preserve only the abstract lines of the flower. Sometimes this extreme conventional treatment is employed merely as a sign of vegetable life, as occasionally in old stained glass, where it is used to signify that the action took place out of doors. In early needlework this archaic treatment is to be found, and is there perfectly appropriate, but with our improved appliances it is now scarcely permissible, except where a certain space is left in a geometrical pattern, better filled by some symbol of vegetable life than by any closer adherence to nature; or in *applied* work, where the thickness of the material hinders more delicate treatment.

Taking for granted that flowers and leaves are the most suitable objects for embroidery, we shall find that the simplest flowers are the best, as they are those which can be most fully expressed by the fewest lines if in outline, and with the fewest shades if in colour. It will be obvious that double flowers are not suitable; we must be content to embroider wild roses, with their few distinct petals and well-marked centres, leaving to the painter the noble Gloire de Dijon, with its multitude of folded leaves and subtle gradations of colour. Not only should the flowers be single, but also of simple form; what are called old-fashioned flowers are, as a rule, the best; some of our favourite garden flowers are spoiled by over-cultivation, and exotics are usually too complex in form to be rendered with the ease which is so essential to our art.

In order to gain any proficiency in designing, careful studies from nature, of flowers and leaves, buds and seed-vessels, in various positions, should be made, and when a thorough acquaintance with natural forms has been gained, designs may be constructed from these drawings. Such practice will lead to a right perception as to what detail must be dispensed with and what retained. Some experience, also, as to what is and what is not practicable with the needle must also be acquired before a satisfactory design can be made. At first we are nearly certain to err by attempting too much. For instance, the crimped petals of the iris, or the jagged edges of the Chinese pink, must be in some measure simplified even in the most careful drawing, and thus made more easy to reduce again from the drawing to the point of simplicity required by the needle. In some flowers the crinkled edges must be entirely left out, as in the pansy, where it is better to take the general curve and shape of the petal than to attempt the little irregularities that are not essential to its character. Where they are essential, as in the pink, they ought to be suggested.

As the object of household decoration is to make our rooms pleasant places of rest, a certain breadth and repose should be aimed at in our work; all sense of fatigue should be avoided. This must be done by being careful not to crowd the design with detail, even though we may be tempted to do so by our command of materials and of the requisite time and patience. The flowers composing a design should not overlap each other too much, for as there is no shadow, the relief is necessarily so low that a sense of crowding and confusion is very easily produced. The appearance of ease must be produced, not only by the expression of freedom in the design and facility in carrying it out, but also by the obviousness of the intention. Detail should be kept subordinate to the design viewed as a whole, and should rather be discovered by degrees than be apparent at the first glance; if this be not attended to, the general effect of the design will be lost, and confusion instead of unity will be the result. Be temperate, therefore, in detail; a thorn here and there on a rose stem will be enough to suggest the thorny character of roses, nor is it needful to make more than a few of the serrations on the leaves; to do more would be to lose the outline, which, of all things, must be preserved distinct.

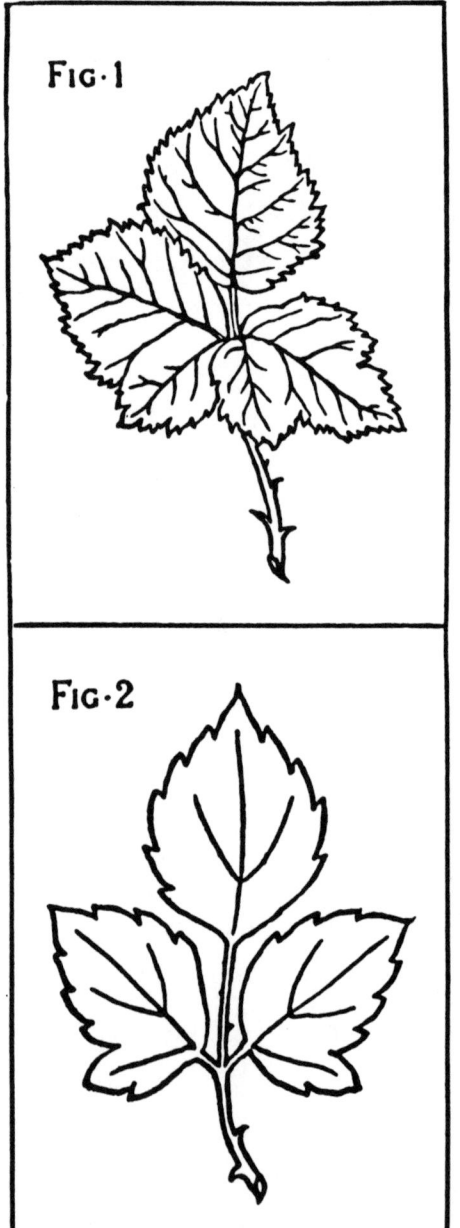

ON DESIGN.

In drawing a leaf, observe carefully its distinguishing characteristics, first as to its general shape, then its growth, whether upright or drooping; then as to detail of form, whether it be serrated or not; if it be, whether finely or coarsely. If the notches be very fine, the edges may be left quite smooth in working; but if they be large and regular, they should be represented, though not in their full number, so as merely to suggest the fact. Fig. 1 shows a bramble leaf carefully drawn from nature; Fig. 2 shows the same leaf sufficiently modified in its details to be embroidered without losing its character; it might be still further conventionalised if the nature of the material or the character of the design required it.

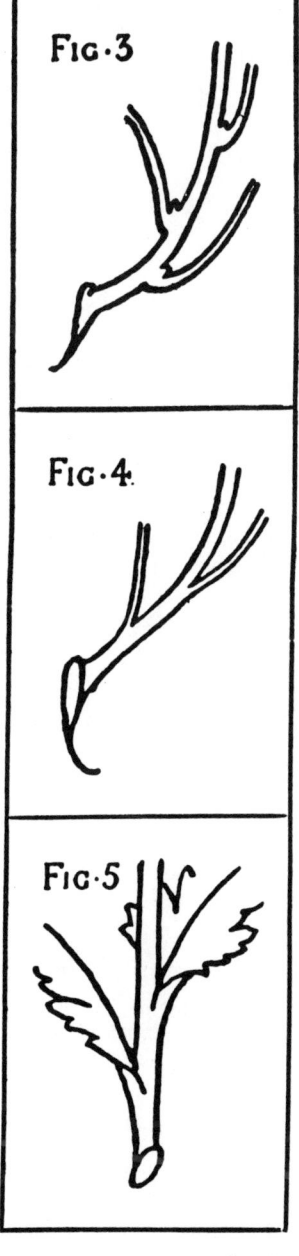

There is another truth that is often neglected, yet which may be expressed without risk of over-multiplying detail—that is, the junction of the leaf and the stalk. This should never be overlooked if the design be meant for outline work, in which, being without the help of colour, we should more fully insist upon truth of line. It should be clearly shown whether the junction be effected by a lobe (as in Fig. 3), or without (as in Fig. 4), or if there be no clear leaf-stalk at all (as in Fig. 5). Also, pains should be taken to finish off the stalks carefully; there are various ways of doing this (see Figs. 3, 4, and 5). It is in these little matters that truth and life may be preserved without risk of confusion, and they help to secure a satisfactory result.

Many instances could be named of glaring inaccuracies to be met with in patterns and decorations—such as a strawberry leaf attached to a carnation flower, a poppy bud opening at the wrong end, or a convolvulus furnished with tendrils. Observation and intelligence will always secure us from mistakes such as these, which are inadmissible as against nature. Departures from nature should never be made through ignorance; to conventionalise is not to depart from nature, it is but to select and use the forms and detail necessary and suitable for our purpose. If we cannot tell the whole truth, let us at least tell no falsehood.

A little practice in simple flower-forms will soon give confidence enough to make more formally arranged patterns, and, as a first step in that direction, some flower, say the honeysuckle or the rose, may be twisted and turned artfully so as to fill the required space, still preserving its natural characteristics. It must be remembered that, however conventionally the flower is treated, its general characteristics must always be preserved. For instance, it would be against all truth to twist into running scrolls the stiff sunflower or the upright sword-lily; their stiff and upright character should rather be insisted upon than hinted at: if grace be the object, a more pliant flower can easily be chosen.

The daisy-shaped flowers are all good for embroidery; being clear and well-defined, they require but little conventionalising. In arranging them—the sunflower, for instance—the petals need not be stiffened into a geometrical star, unless the flowers are to be associated with some scroll-work that demands rigid treatment. In nature, the sunflower petals are too long to stand out evenly round

ON DESIGN.

the black disc; this tendency to droop should be just indicated here and there in the design (see Fig. 6).

The daffodil and narcissus, and the lily tribes, work extremely well; so do the primrose, potentilla, and wild rose. There are also many berries that make beautiful combinations with their blossoms and leaves, as the bramble, cherry, &c. There is no need for a full list; so soon as the task of designing has become familiar, it will be known at a glance whether a flower be likely to be effective or not, and it will be found that the simplest flowers fulfil most completely the requirements of the art.

In designs for *filled-in* embroidery, the vacant spaces should be larger than they need be for outline work, especially if the work is to be done in crewels, for the substance of the wool fills up the spaces, and contracts the material a little; so that a design which looks a little bald on paper will prove sufficiently handsome when worked.

Designs for *outline* work may be closer in arrangement; they should be very carefully drawn, as all the beauty of outline work consists in its grace and truth of form. This style, by allowing more grace, allows also in some respects more naturalism;

but no attempt at roundness of form should be made, beyond what can be attained by simple curves without shading. Such details as the junction of leaf and stalk and the correct veining of the leaves should be insisted on. The careful drawing of leaf-veins imparts life and curvature to an outline that otherwise has no meaning.

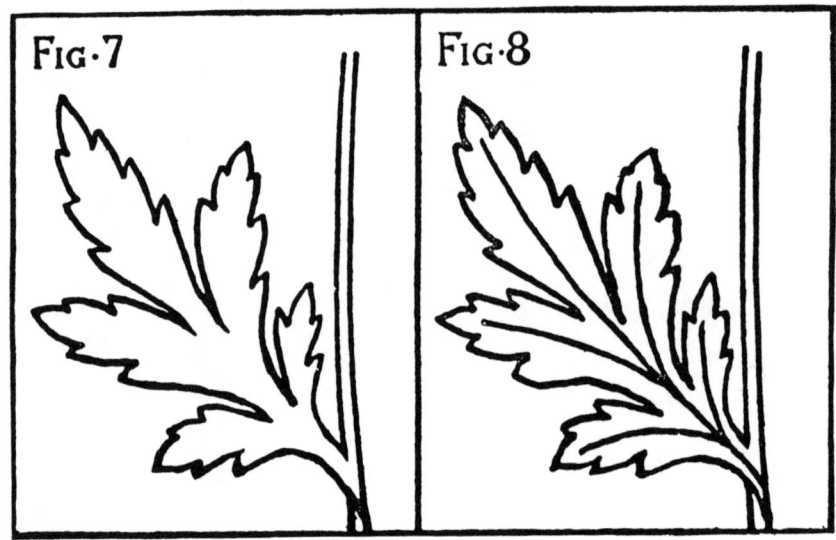

Fig. 7 shows a leaf of the common scarlet poppy conventionalised for working in outline without veins; Fig. 8 shows the same leaf with the veins added. It will be seen how much life and vigour depend on this simple veining.

In designing a border, it must be taken into consideration whether it be intended for a horizontal or a perpendicular position. In some cases, of course, the upright arrangement will run no risk of being used horizontally, in others there is less certainty. There are borders which may be used either way, and there are others which, at first sight, seem as if they might be used indiscriminately, but after a little study are found to be more suitable for one position than the other.

Borders designed for a horizontal position, and composed of upright sprigs, single or grouped, require a line or two below, serving to keep them together; without this they look disjointed, and each sprig is too independent of the rest. It is not necessary for the flowers to spring from this line, which has the same controlling power whether they touch it or not. Should the sprigs be large, a single line is not enough; a series of lines should be arranged. These will balance the composition, giving weight to the lower part, and making a pleasing opposition of line. Scroll borders also are often improved by a line on each side; it is not an unvarying necessity, but in many cases a great improvement. Sometimes the effect is obtained by the scroll or border being worked on a narrow piece of material, and then sewn on to some other stuff of a different shade; in this case the enclosing lines are obtained by the limit of the material on which the border is worked.

It is often necessary to enlarge flowers, such as the daisy and primrose, beyond their natural size; this is no sin against truth or good taste, so long as regard is had to their proportion to each other when grouped. If a sunflower is reduced to a size suitable for the space at command, it must not be associated with daffodils enlarged to fit the same place; their relative proportions must be maintained, or an unnatural appearance is the result.

Good conventional work is always truthful, and yet it ought always to maintain a certain reticence, which may occasionally amount to a severe reserve, by the expression only of the most general features. Reticence there should always be, allowing no extravagance or waste, no useless or superfluous lines.

Hitherto we have only spoken of flower-forms for embroidery, but there are other natural forms which can be associated with them.

Birds and butterflies are often most effective; they give animation to the design, and are useful aids in the general composition, as they may be placed where they are necessary for the balance of the design, or for relief in colour, which it would be difficult to attain by other means. Butterflies are especially appropriate, as, from their variety of size and colour, they can be made to harmonise with almost any grouping of flowers. We should avoid mixing birds or butterflies of one climate with flowers peculiar to another.

Ribbon twisted or knotted round the stems of flowers, or tying up garlands, makes also a pleasant variety, but requires experience and judgment in its use. Care should be taken not to twist the ribbon into impossible bows, nor to allow it to hang in too wavy and straggling lines.

Vases can also be occasionally introduced; they are best represented by some material laid on, or else worked in lines only, giving the outline and the pattern on it, as in a pencil drawing without shading.

Good designs may be produced after some study of the kind indicated in this chapter, no more naturalism being used than can be expressed with the materials consistently with clearness of outline and a due feeling of repose. Half—perhaps more than half—the object will then be accomplished, for the principles which have guided us hitherto may still be applied in adding the colour that will make our work true art, and a delight to the eye so long as a fragment of it lasts.

CHAPTER III.

ON COLOUR.

FTER good design, good colouring comes next in importance, and is so essential to a piece of embroidery that, while harmonious colouring may atone even for faulty design, a good design will certainly be spoiled by vulgar colouring. As the colouring of our work is a matter of so much consequence, we cannot be too particular in considering it well beforehand, that all may be in harmony and in keeping, not only with itself, but with the purpose and position for which it is intended.

We have already seen that our work is not to be a mere copy of Nature, but rather a skilful adaptation of her forms to decorative purposes. And as conventionalism in form is imposed upon us as a necessity, it also follows that the same necessity has to be observed in our imitation of nature with regard to colour. This becomes apparent from the very outset. In many cases it is utterly impossible to give the natural colouring of a particular flower; we may, perhaps, be able to get its general tone, but the subtle gradations which are with difficulty reproduced in painting are quite out of reach in embroidery. As a simple instance, take a blue pansy: the first difficulty will be to get silk or wool dyed the proper shades; but supposing that overcome, a greater one will arise—that of mingling the tints, with all the delicacies of tone and intermixture of shade that are found in the flower, without producing a confused and unsatisfactory effect; and after our utmost efforts to represent a pansy as it appears in nature, the result is sure to be a failure. And if this be the case with a flower so simply coloured as the pansy, how much greater the difficulty will be with flowers of more complex hues!

But there is another consideration. It must be remembered how different are the surroundings of flowers, as used for decorative effect either in painting or embroidery, from their surroundings in the open air. Therefore, in adapting their colour to their place in in-door decoration, their more subdued tints and less brilliant aspect should be chosen; for their brighter colours have the clear air, the sunlight, their natural texture, and, above all, their evanescence, to render them delightful. The pure colour alone, without these aids, transferred to needlework, would be glaring and gaudy. Moreover, as there is no raw colour in nature, but an admixture of yellow in most of her hues, it is a great mistake to render her brilliancy, which is chiefly owing to subtle qualities of texture, by raw and gaudy silks and wools, which smite the eye without pleasing the sense. Thus, as it is impossible to reproduce the fluctuating iridescence of the natural flower, it is better to take nature as a suggestive guide rather than as a pattern for servile copying, and to choose colours with regard to their general harmony rather than their separate exact truth to nature.

Embroidery is a decorative work, and therefore must be regulated by the rules of decorative treatment; and as harmony is one of the first considerations, the attempt to combine a close imitation of

ON COLOUR.

nature in *colour* with conventionalism in *form* would be a fatal error. Consistency of treatment must be aimed at, and having simplified the forms of nature, we must, for corresponding reasons, simplify the colours also.

The colour of the ground of a piece of work must regulate its general tone. Some *one* prevailing colour should be adopted, and the rest chosen with reference to it. In many instances this colour has to be decided by the ultimate destination of the work, as in the case of *portières*, or window curtains, which must be in keeping with the rest of the furniture of the room. But supposing the piece of work to be complete in itself, the colour of the ground is first chosen, and then taken as a guide to the colours of the flowers to be embroidered upon it.

The colours chosen must not be in contrast, but in harmony. Thus if the ground be green, pure yellows and pure blues will harmonise, while red will produce a violent contrast; green being composed of blue and yellow, either of its component parts will agree with it. Some of the most beautifully coloured work is that done in one key of colour; that is, one colour is taken as the key-note, and those shades only are used that form its component parts, or that have the original colour in their composition.

For instance, in embroidery on gold-coloured satin, nothing will look so well as a design coloured in shades of russet and golden browns, every now and then striking, as it were, the higher or lower octave of the key-note by the introduction of a lighter or darker shade of the pure ground colour. Again, taking green for the ground and treating it in the same way, it has first to be considered whether it is a yellow or blue green. If a yellow green, the highest note should then be yellow. The same harmony should be carried through the brown, warm, and russet greens, up to the primary colour, yellow, to which all these tints owe their warmth, and which is the chief constituent of the ground. But if the ground be a blue green, colder greens must be used, of a sage rather than russet tint, while the key-note is struck with a pure blue, that being the chief constituent part of the ground colour, and also the cool element in the other colours used. Worked under this careful restraint, the resulting effect, subdued though it be, is abundantly gratifying.

The combination of a greater variety of colours is not so easy. Contrasting colours require great care and judgment in their arrangement, and should be made by their rarity to add brilliancy to the surrounding harmony. If contrasting colours are placed side by side, the brilliancy of each is certainly enhanced, yet the result is not harmonious, but harsh and disturbing. Contrasting colours, however, are capable of producing good effects, but in managing them so much judgment and discretion is necessary, that it is best to be on the safe side and avoid them, until we have attained such a degree of experience as may warrant a flight into these more difficult regions. Place a pure blue near a pure yellow, and the effect is crude and bad; but slightly tone the blue with yellow, and the yellow with blue, and instantly the effect becomes pleasing. In the same manner a strong blue and a bright red with a dash of yellow in it are harsh; but introduce in their neighbourhood a subdued russet-green—the tertiary tint, a combination of the three—and a softer, more pleasing effect is imparted.

Pale soft tints are more easily combined than strong deep colours. If we would avoid vulgar colouring, we shall do well not to introduce more than two of the primary colours, in their purity, into one piece of work; the subordinate parts, as leaves and stalks or scroll work, must be more or less of neutral tints—olive, russet, and soft brown shades. Purples and tints inclining to blue are difficult to manage. Of the three primary colours, blue—the cold one in nature—pleases us, not by its coldness, but by its purity. The secondary tints, green and purple, lose tone in proportion to the amount of blue they contain, a preponderance of which adds to their coldness and hardness. In the tertiary tints, those that have the smallest proportion of blue in them are to be preferred; as russet, which is one part blue, one part yellow, and two parts red; and olive, which is one part blue, two parts yellow, and one part red: these are both more pleasing than slate, which is two parts blue, one part yellow, and one part red.

It is not a bad rule to make the colour that forms the larger constituent part of the ground the chief pure colour used in the design, even when one key of colour is not otherwise strictly carried out as explained above. Thus, where the ground is a *red* plum or maroon, pure red pinks—that is, pinks without any shade of blue in them—will harmonise satisfactorily and be much more pleasing than if blue—the lesser element of the ground colour—be used; but if the ground be of a *blue* plum colour, pale blue would be more pleasing than pink, blue being the leading colour in the ground.

We will describe a piece of silk embroidery in which this plan of colour was most charmingly carried out. The ground was bronze-green satin; upon it were worked sprays of convolvulus springing from a vase of grey satin; the convolvulus flowers were white, edged with a pure blue—not the purplish blue of the natural flower, for that would not have harmonised so well—and yet there was nothing unnatural in the effect of the colour. The leaves were of yellow and grey greens, and the stalks a brownish green. Then, to give warmth and life, some sulphur butterflies hovered over the garlands. Thus, though in the colouring of the design the component parts only of the bronze green ground were used, the effect was perfect. This piece of work was for the front of an upright piano, and its quiet cheerfulness replaced with admirable effect the usual unmeaning fretwork lined with silk of some raw colour. Colour is so much a matter of feeling, and of so subtle a nature, that only the most general rules can be safely given, and even these more as guides than as laws to be implicitly obeyed. Shades and tones are so varied and uncertain that it is impossible to describe them in words; the eye must be educated to appreciate them, and to learn their combinations and effects, which in the description may be so easily misapprehended. A master of colour will produce harmonies where, with the same materials, another would produce discords. In the Bellini picture in the National Gallery, "S. Jerome in his Study," the prevailing colours are red, blue, and green; but instead of a vulgar glaring effect, such as would have been produced by an ordinary hand, a most delicious harmony is the result—warm, glowing, and yet subdued, owing to the judicious choice of tones and their varying intensity.

It is often said that the old-fashioned colours are the best; this is so because they are softer and purer than the brilliant colours which have vitiated the taste of later years. Metallic aniline dyes—the discovery of which was hailed as a blessing, but which the artist looks upon in quite another light—are harsh and unlike anything in nature; take them into the sunlit garden, where a flower, however brilliant, is never raw in colour, and you will feel the discord instantly. However strong they may be, they have no depth about them; they smite your eye, they do not draw your gaze into them. It would seem as if all their strength existed literally on the surface only, so soon do the aniline dyes fade. In a modern Turkey carpet, which has been coloured with modern hues to suit the English taste, the colour soon goes out of the bluish magenta-crimson that has been used instead of the old pure red, and only a dirty pinkish-white is left.

That the pure colours produced from vegetable dyes last longer and preserve their original harmony by fading all together, when they do fade with the lapse of years, is a strong argument in their favour; for nothing is more provoking than to find work that has cost time and thought rendered discordant and ugly by the colour having gone completely from some of the shades, and remaining in full brightness in others. Everything must grow old and fade away in time; but old age, even in needlework, may still be rendered beautiful if all its tints fade together, instead of dying by piecemeal.

A simple and very effective arrangement of colour, and one especially appropriate for outline work, is one in which the pattern is worked on a dark ground in a lighter shade of the same. If the curtains be dark crimson and the pattern worked in a lighter shade, the material is enriched and relieved sufficiently without the introduction of colours, possibly unsuitable to the general harmony of the room. In a small room, curtains embroidered in many colours do not look well, unless, perhaps, where the ground is unbleached linen or some similar light-coloured substance; but by working a sprig or other design in outline in a brighter shade of the dark material, the heaviness of a mass of self-colour is much relieved. Outline embroidery, also, looks extremely well when done in a dark colour on a light ground —either a darker shade of the same colour as the ground, or an altogether different colour, as dark blue on unbleached linen or raw silk; dark red and brown also look extremely well on the unbleached tints. In outline patterns, to be worked in not only a different shade but in a different colour from the ground, a greater contrast is required, and the lines, though thin, should be strong.

If at any time it be found that the ground colour chosen is too obtrusive and does not retire enough, a little diaper pattern may be worked all over the piece in a darker shade of the ground; this gives depth and richness, and lends greater value to the principal design. In cases, too, where the plain ground is felt to be monotonous, the diaper may be used with good effect. A simple little pattern is all that is necessary, for the diaper must never obtrude itself, either by its elaborate pattern or strength of colour—like a healthy influence, it should be felt rather than seen.

As a rule, dark grounds give the strongest relief to the design. Dark brownish greens, deep dull blues, and rich maroon shades, make good grounds; but if the design be many-coloured, black will be found the safest, as it will subdue, and at the same time show out, the brilliancy. Some of the most beautiful work is done on pale grounds; creamy white, buff, pale grey and fawn, all make good ground-tones. If strong relief is desired, either a dark or a light ground must be chosen; the intermediate shades, unless of a very neutral tone, do not as a rule make good grounds—great judgment is required in their use, or an indistinct effect is the result.

It will help much to preserve the unity and clearness of the effect if all the different shades of the design contrast more with the ground than with each other. Thus, if the ground be dark, all the colours of the design should be of lighter shades than the ground colour; if the ground be light, the whole design should show dark upon it.

Keeping in mind that repose is a most important element in art decoration, we must be content with a few colours at a time. Just as we may not crowd in details of form, so we must be sparing in details of colour, nor must we attempt every shade and gradation of tone. Let us be content with the hint that Nature gives us. If we must embroider a blue flower, let us choose such a blue as will harmonise with the rest of the work rather than try to match the exact hue of nature, and shade it just so far as will give a clear idea of the flower without relief or projection. As a general rule, two shades are enough (unless the flower be unusually large) to convey sufficient detail without confusion: let us not attempt all the shades and mixed tints to be found in nature, or we shall spoil our work, making it confused and indistinct, neither conveying a good idea of what was intended, nor producing the repose of decorative treatment. We must make up our mind, once for all, that it is impossible to imitate nature closely with embroidery materials; therefore, in utilising her beauties for decorative work, we must conventionalise them in colour as well as in form, so as to produce a work of art, instead of some nondescript "fancy work" that is neither art nor nature.

In those cases where a natural treatment can be followed in form, a corresponding treatment will probably be possible in colour; and so long as such treatment is consistent with repose, harmony, and clearness in design and apprehension, it may be safely adopted; but it must be borne in mind that to follow nature closely in one flower and to conventionalise another in the same design is to destroy harmony: all must be in keeping—naturalised or conventionalised in exactly the same degree.

CHAPTER IV.

ON MATERIALS AND STITCHES.

WE have now to give a few suggestions as to the materials and stitches best suited to the kinds of needlework of which we have been speaking.

In the material on which to work there is great liberty of choice; silk, satin, velvet, cloth, and linen have all their appropriate uses. The first thing to be considered is the suitability of the material in texture and substance to the purpose for which it is intended. For instance, delicate satin is not appropriate for a "tidy" intended to be washed and constantly renewed; nor is rough serge or coarse linen suited for a dainty screen or cushion that is to form a lasting ornament.

The next thing to remember is that the material should suit the work that is to be put upon it. The material used for ornamenting should be superior, or at least equal in quality to the material ornamented. Coarse worsteds are suited to rough serge or thick linen; finer worsteds, crewel (which is two-thread worsted), and filosel (which is inferior silk), to finer linen or cloth; while silk and satin require silks of the finest and brightest texture. Crewel should not be used for embroidery on silk, satin, or velvet, though silk looks well on fine woollen material or on linen.

Another point is that the material on which we work should be good and true of its kind, well and evenly woven, well dyed, and of a fast colour; and if there be any pattern, such as diaper or twill, upon it, it should be fairly produced by weaving, and not by dressing or stamping.

For working in crewel, we recommend unbleached linen, and woollen fabrics, such as cloth, serge, and some other materials now used for ladies' dresses. Mixed stuffs, such as those made of wool and silk, or wool and cotton, should be looked on with suspicion, as not likely to be durable enough to repay the time spent upon them, and also as being liable to shrink and wrinkle with heat or damp. Thick diagonal cloth, or serge, as it is sometimes called, makes a very good substance to work upon either with silk or crewel, and is useful for large pieces of household work. It looks well for curtains, as it is not so heavy as broadcloth, and it is easier to work upon—a great merit, as the labour of a large piece of work is more than doubled if the material be too thick or close for the needle to pass through without a twitch or pull. Serge is also useful for table-covers, bracket borders, and many other things.

Very fine and highly-dressed cloth is not so good as serge, or even as cloth of a flannel-like surface; indeed, no glazed nor highly-dressed material makes a good ground—the stitches lie too much on the surface, or stand out from it, instead of forming a part of it. Satin, however, embroidered with soft bright silks, is the exception to this rule, because by these a perfect harmony of texture is obtained.

There are many differences of opinion about the best linen for crewel embroidery, and a thoroughly satisfactory kind is difficult to meet with. The fancy-work shops recommend a material made on purpose, usually called "Verona crash;" it is close, rough, and hard, its most engaging quality being its colour. But as roughness and coarseness should not be sought for their own sake, we strongly advise our readers to choose their linen at an ordinary linendraper's, and to avoid the special materials made to supply a passing fashion. The old hand-loom linens would be the best if we could get them, the warp and woof are more even and canvas-like, and they are less dressed for sale than modern linens; but, failing these, it is best to turn over the stock of linen at some good household shop, and we shall be very unfortunate if we do not find something to suit our purpose. The shops in the North of England afford the best choice, and an opportunity of choosing linen in any Flemish town should not be neglected.

The names given to different sorts of linen vary in different places, but we have found that glass-towelling and Barnsley pillow linen—the more unbleached the better—are best for tidies and smaller pieces of work. "Barnsley loom" linen is good in colour, bright in the thread, and evenly woven, but heavier than the pillow linen; while for strong coarse work, such as bed hangings, Barnsley sheeting and Russia towelling are useful. The best kind of "Russia duck"— not the "duck" sailors use, but a superior kind of roller towelling—is a good material, yellow and even, and, though strong, not unseemly. Some of the unglazed hollands are good in colour and texture; in fact, any linen may be used that appears suitable to the purpose and good of its kind, and without the thick threads that are unsightly if left in, and make holes if taken out. For crewel work, the linen should be just coarse enough to allow the worsted to pass through without difficulty.

In the choice of materials, we must not allow ourselves to be led away against our own better judgment by what is said at the fancy-work shop to be "the proper thing now," or to take what is given to us, whether it be to our taste or not. An independent choice of material leads to individuality in our work, which is always a great charm; and if we do not design our own patterns—it is not everyone who can—we must guard the more jealously such choice as is left to us. By reserving this choice of materials, we free ourselves from the thraldom of the workshops, and of people too much interested in the sale of these special materials while the fashion lasts to give good advice.

We do not consider cotton a good material for embroidery; it does not bear washing so well as linen, and it is not so durable. We have a fragment of embroidery in fine crimson silk, part of a coverlet, probably a hundred years old; the flower patterns are very beautiful, and the needlework is marvellous; the silk is almost perfect, but the ground, a twilled cotton, is not only worn, but stretched, soft, and rotten. Linen, with equal wear, might have been threadbare, but would have kept its shape and colour. Some cotton materials, however, may be advantageously used; one is cotton velvet, or velveteen, which is firm and durable, and often dyed in good shades not to be found in silk; it is also useful for several purposes, such as chair cushions, which, if made of silk velvet, would be soon crushed and spoiled. Another exception is Bolton (or "work-house") sheeting, which is very thick, unbleached, and twilled. We have seen this worked in filosel for curtains, and it may be used for bed hangings or coverlets worked in worsted or crewel, or with an *appliqué* pattern in serge. The very best kind should be chosen, and it should not have too much time or labour spent upon it in the working. Being inexpensive, it is useful for

ON MATERIALS AND STITCHES.

an experiment, as a pattern may be quickly worked upon it in one colour to try if it be effective and well-balanced, before carrying it out on a more costly material.

We now come to the stitches, which, though difficult to explain clearly in words, are really simple and few—the simpler and the fewer, the better the work.

The most useful stitch is the embroidery or long stitch, known to canvas-workers as the *tent stitch*. A single line of it is like the wrong side of back stitching in plain needlework, only the stitches are longer. In Fig. 9, supposing the work to be in a frame, we bring the needle up at 1 and put it down at 2, bring it up again at 3 and put it down at 4, and so on. In outline work the thread should be kept to the left of the needle, and great care should be taken to bring the needle up exactly in the line of the pattern, or a wavy uncertain line will be the result, and the character of the pattern will be lost. If the work be done in the hand, as is best for outline work, the easiest and quickest way is to work this stitch upwards, or from the worker (Fig. 10). The needle should be brought through at 1, and put it in again from 2 to 3, and from 4 to 5, and so on. We must be careful that the stitches are neither too tight nor too loose, that the curves are not "broken-backed," and that the points are clear and sharp.

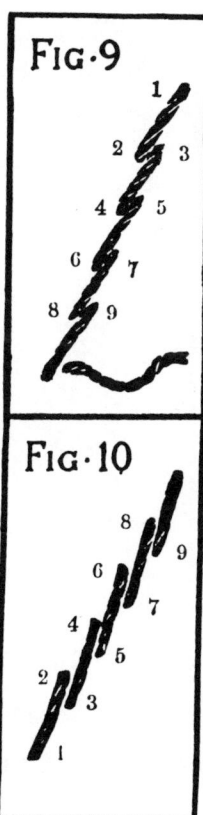

In working thickly filled-in embroidery, it is better not to outline the flower or leaf first, as their shape is not bounded by an outline in nature, and in this kind of work a more natural appearance is aimed at than in outline work. The stitches are to express the form of the leaf, and they should take the direction that the lines would take if we were shading the flower or leaf with a pen or pencil. For instance, in working a pansy, the stitches in each leaf must take the direction of the lines in Fig. 11, and not cross the petals as in Fig. 12. In a simple leaf the stitches should form the same angle with the middle rib that the lateral veins do in the real leaf, as in Fig. 13. Leaves having parallel veins, such as the jonquil, should be worked in parallel stitches (Fig. 14). In working the petals of flowers this rule cannot always be carried out, but it is often possible, and will be found to give great life and vigour to the work. The meeting of the stitches at the point of a snowdrop petal will express an important part of its construction in a perfectly simple and legitimate manner. (We would remind our readers in this place of the value of the accurate drawings from nature recommended in Chapter II.) It will be found that in the proper placing of stitches in the filling-in of flowers, and in the exercise of the judgment in all these particulars, the difference between skilled and 'prentice work, between the intelligent use of the needle and mere mechanical copying, will be evident.

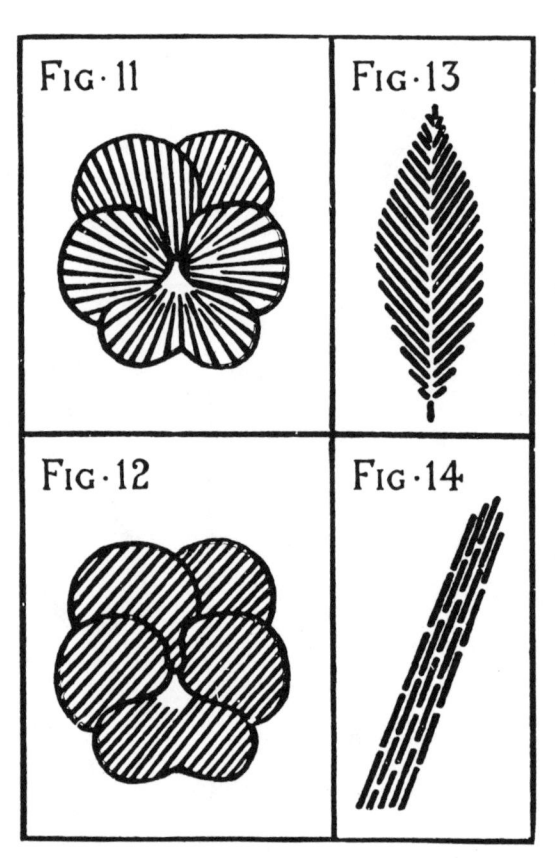

In working narrow leaves, where one stitch may reach from the middle to the edge of the leaf, it is best to pass the thread from the edge underneath to the middle, thus beginning each stitch in the middle and making the under side almost like the upper. The thread must not be pulled so tight as to pucker the work. A broad leaf or petal requires more than one stitch between the middle and the edge, and for these the needle may be brought up again whenever the next stitch seems wanted; but two stitches together should not begin nor end on the same line, except on the outside edge to preserve the outline, or in showing the middle rib.

Unless the embroidery be very large and bold, the line formed by the meeting of the stitches evenly down the middle of a leaf will sufficiently mark the mid-rib. If in the real leaf it be very deep and well-defined, a minute space left between the two lines, very narrow near the stalk and tapering till the threads meet again near the point, will in most cases be sufficient. As a general rule, lateral veins need not be indicated at all; if they be very marked in the natural leaf, and either raised, or of a decidedly different colour from the leaf itself, they may be laid on by applying a cord or piece of thick silk-twist and fastening it down with small stitches of fine silk of the same colour. This way of marking the veins is only appropriate to large and rather coarse pieces of work; in fine work it is apt to attract the eye too much and to make the veins unduly prominent; in most cases the meeting of the stitches down the middle of the leaf is enough. If it be necessary to make the veins of another shade of colour, and also to indicate the lateral veins, it is best to work the leaf first without regarding them, and to put them in afterwards over the work, in the usual embroidery stitch of the desired shade.

F

As to the proper length of the embroidery stitch, it is obvious that no rule can be given; it depends both on the general style of the work, and on the shape and size of the flower or leaf. In the embroidered marks in the corners of old-fashioned blankets—always worthy of notice for their pattern—stitches of two or three inches long were used with good effect for the purpose; while in some fine embroidery, stitches two-or-three-eighths of an inch long are the longest that can be found. For ordinary crewel embroidery the stitches may be from three-eighths to half-an-inch long, varied to suit their position, some being necessarily short; in silk work they will be rather shorter. It should be remembered that a long stitch gives ease and smoothness to the work, while a short one, though it may look painstaking, has an air of timidity that belongs rather to the work of the beginner than of the practised needlewoman.

Satin-stitch, worked over and under so that both sides are alike, hardly needs mention; it is only a way of using the long-stitch for white work or for filled-in work, where the direction of the stitches has not to be considered.

Chain-stitch is sometimes used for filled-in embroidery; the lines of the chain are laid very close together, and follow the form of the leaf till it is filled in, beginning at the outside and working to the centre. Some Algerian and Eastern work is done entirely in this stitch; it is found frequently in ancient crewel-work—still we do not recommend it; it has a slightly mechanical effect, and can be perfectly imitated with the sewing-machine; it is also less elastic and less easily adapted to varying forms than the long-stitch, which is the true embroidery stitch. The chain-stitch is sometimes useful for outline work where a stronger line is required than that made by the long-stitch; it may be used very effectively in the horizontal

ON MATERIALS AND STITCHES.

lines that we have recommended as a base for single flowers to spring from, or for enclosing a narrow border.

For these two last purposes a good effect may be made by enclosing an arrangement of short diagonal and perpendicular lines between horizontal ones. Suggestions for these may often be found on Oriental china, where some rich-looking border proves on examination to be only a few long and short lines skilfully arranged. We insert a few specimens by way of example.

The *herring-bone stitch* was formerly much used. We have seen an old piece of fine linen embroidered all over with a bold and graceful design of flowers in outline, in pale gold-coloured silk; here and there a piece is filled in, to give accent and distinctness to the design, and the stems are worked in a close herring-bone stitch, which gives them a strength and substance that would be wanting if so bold and spreading a pattern were worked simply in outline. We possess another piece, part of a quilt, probably half-a-century older, which is worked in the same colour and material. The ground is thickly quilted in back-stitch, in a scale pattern, and a conventional flower design is worked on it in herring-bone stitch, done so closely as to resemble braid.

In the first of these two examples some of the filled-in work is done in a peculiar manner—from side to side. Supposing an oval leaf to be filled in, it is begun at the base, where it is very narrow, with a few satin stitches; then, when space enough is reached, instead of passing the thread all the way underneath to the opposite side, about one-third of the width of the leaf is taken up in the needle, and the next stitch is done in the same manner on the opposite side of the leaf, working from side to side until the leaf becomes too narrow again, when it is finished with a few satin stitches. This stitch throws all the silk to the top, and the crossing of the threads in the middle of the leaf has a very rich and soft effect, giving also the appearance of a vein.

The *French knot* is a useful device for the centres of such flowers as the daisy or sunflower, or for the ends of the stamens of some other flowers. It is made by bringing the thread through to the front of the work, and holding the thread in the left hand four or five inches from the work, the needle being in the right hand; the thread in the left hand is twisted two or three times round the needle as close to the work as possible, then the point is turned down into the material, nearly, but not exactly, where the thread came up; the needle is pulled through to the other side, and the thread drawn carefully till the knot is firm. Care must be taken to draw the thread round the needle close up to the work before the needle is pulled quite through, lest the knot should hang loose and the effect be spoiled.

Some Eastern embroidery is done in the long stitch first described; it is worked in regular lines across the shape to be filled, no attempt being made to follow the natural lines of the flower or leaf. This looks well for purely conventional forms, but is not appropriate for a design of natural flowers; it resembles *applied* work in treatment, and the shapes are usually enclosed with a gold or black line.

There are other stitches that may be sometimes used with good effect, but they are, as a rule, only modifications of the more generally useful ones that we have described. Every worker has her own devices for getting over difficulties or giving effect to her work, suggested by the necessity of the moment or the peculiarity of her materials—devices that, according to their success, show the skill of the workwoman; but we recommend the beginner to make herself well versed in the use of ordinary stitches before trying novelties.

CHAPTER V.

ON METHODS AND USES.

AS the kinds of work we have described cannot be purchased at the shops ready for the needle, and as it is difficult, if not impossible, to have the design we have made traced satisfactorily on the material by another hand, we will give a few directions for making these useful preparations. The trouble that must be taken will be well repaid by the great gain to the work in intelligence and individuality.

Outline embroidery and crewel work on linen may be done in the hand—most people can work with skill enough to avoid puckering an outline—but a frame must be used for delicate materials, such as silk, satin, or velvet, which would be spoiled if creased, and also for heavy embroidery on a slight material.

For these delicate fabrics it is a good plan to have the frame edged with strong linen or tape nailed to it, and to sew the satin or silk very closely to this, instead of sewing the material itself round the rollers of the frame and lacing it at the sides. This latter plan does very well for cloth or serge, but silk or velvet will not always bear the stretching. Sometimes it is more convenient to pin the work into the frame, especially when only a portion of the material requires stretching—the corners of a table-cloth, for instance. Then we have to guard against marking the inner sides of the stuff, and pins will mark it less than stitches.

It is always worth while to arrange and prepare work well before beginning; a little trouble at first saves a great deal of vexation afterwards. "Well begun is half done," and when the first stitch is put into a piece of work that has been well thought out and carefully designed, the materials well chosen and in sufficient quantities, the ground fixed exactly and truly into the frame, and the pattern neatly drawn out, we may well feel that the work is half done—certainly it is the lighter and pleasanter part that lies before us, and we have made success all but certain.

The necessity of care in keeping the work from dust while it is in hand, and scrupulous cleanliness in the working, is too obvious to be insisted upon; but it may be suggested that, in working a piece too long to put all at once into the frame, it is a good plan to place a layer of cotton-wool and tissue paper over the part that is finished, when it comes to be rolled up, lest the thick part of the work should impress marks upon the ground.

We have spoken before of the necessity of simplicity, remembering that decorative effect, not a flower-painting, is to be produced; but we must give one more warning—work should not be shaded so as to produce roundness or raised effect inconsistent with legitimate aims, still less should any attempt be made to raise it by stuffing it with wadding, by thick stitches of coarse cotton, or any such horrible devices.

Silk is so easily caught and dragged that great care is required in working it. To prevent it from twisting, it is best to have a flat bodkin or stiletto at hand to hold under the silk as it is drawn through; and when the work is finished, it is a good plan to rub a little very stiff, almost dry, paste or gum into the back of the embroidery: this will hold all the ends firmly, and prevent the stitches from being drawn or pulled from the wrong side. It is better to rub on the paste with the finger than with a brush, as it can be done more lightly and with less danger of pressing it through to the right side; some tissue paper should then be laid over the paste and pressed lightly: this should be done, and have become perfectly dry, before the work is taken out of the frame.

To make linen work smooth and even when it is finished, it should be damped all over at the back with a sponge, and then stretched tightly and evenly, face downwards, on a board, or pinned out on a nailed carpet with a clean cloth underneath it. When the work as well as the linen is quite dry, it may be taken up; and if the edges show the pin-marks, they can be smoothed with the fingers. When linen work is washed, it must be treated in the same way.

Bold *applied* work may be done in the hand, but finer kinds are most easily managed in a frame. Great care should be taken to cut the applied pieces very exactly; the back of each piece may be just touched with gum—as thick and dry as possible, lest it should come through—in order to keep it in its place on the material, which should first be marked with the pattern. The applied piece should then be very carefully smoothed and adjusted, for a curved or cross-cut piece is very apt to get out of its proper curves or to stretch too much. The edges are fastened down by laying a cord of silver or gold twist, or of thick silk, on the edge, and sewing it down with fine stitches. Another way is to sew over the edges with a button-hole stitch worked in a lighter or a darker shade of the colour of the applied piece. If the pattern be of leaves, their veins may be indicated by long stitches in a little lighter or darker shade, which gives a full and rich effect. Applied work is perhaps better suited for purely conventional forms than for flowers; though in large bold work these last are very telling.

The processes for transferring designs from paper to the ground on which they are to be worked vary with the nature and colour of the material. For a light-coloured stuff, the best way is to trace the design on tissue or other thin paper, to lay the material flat upon a table, and fix the place of the pattern upon it very exactly. Then put a piece of carbonised blue or black paper, face downward on the material, between it and the paper pattern, and with a stiletto or other hard-pointed, but not too sharp instrument (a metallic pencil or a knitting needle will often answer the purpose), trace over all the lines of the design, taking care to keep the paper pattern from slipping, and that the fingers do not press so heavily on the transferring paper as to cause the colour to come off unduly.

The ordinary carbonised paper is easily procured, being in common use in shops for writing bills in duplicate. The objection to it is that the colour may come off too readily, and a shade of blue or grey be left on the material, especially if the latter be at all of a rough or woolly texture. Before a new sheet of this paper is used, it should be rubbed gently with a cloth so as to remove any unfixed colour; and an old sheet should be carefully cherished.

A good white transferring paper would be very useful for darker stuffs, but the only kind we have seen is too greasy to be safe for delicate materials. For these, the old-fashioned plan of *pouncing* must be followed, which, if rather more troublesome than tracing, has the advantage of being safe.

For *pouncing*, the design must be drawn on thick paper, and then pricked along the lines with a pin. The paper should be held up to the light to see that the holes are clear and in sufficient number to show the pattern. When the pattern is fixed, face upward, on the material, dust it over with starch tied up in a little muslin, so that the fine powder goes through the holes. Flour or violet powder will answer, and may be best applied about the pattern with a soft brush. This done, the paper must be taken up very carefully, lifting it straight upwards off the material, so that it does not blur the little dots of white, which ought to be in regular order underneath, marking out the design. Some white tracing paint should be ready prepared, which may be made of pipeclay and very weak gum, or of whitening and beer, or in a third way, which we prefer, with whitening and gin or whisky. Perhaps, on the whole, the Chinese white used by water-colour painters, and sold in shilling bottles, is the best. With any of these, and a pen or brush, the lines of the pattern, indicated by the dots of white powder, should be traced, keeping the original design before the eye lest the dots should be misleading or the spirit of the drawing be lost, and blowing away the powder where it has come through too plentifully. Care must be taken not to make the lines too broad, lest they should show under the work, and for this reason the white liquid should not be too thin: it will become whiter and show more plainly as it dries. For a light-coloured material, which might be endangered by the carbonised paper, the pouncing may be done with powder blue, which dusts off again without smearing the stuff as some powdered colours do, and the blue dots should be followed with some coloured ink or paint.

There is still another way, when the design is of such a nature that it can be carried out. This is to cut out the pattern in paper, place it on the material, and trace round the edge with chalk. Then remove the paper and go over the chalk outline with Chinese white perfecting it where it is defective.

It may be necessary to say a word as to the various objects which may be rendered decorative by needlework, though many of these have been already mentioned incidentally. They are well-nigh numberless, from a mat for the coal-box to the most costly hangings; among the rest may be mentioned curtains for doors, windows, and book-cases; chair-covers, cushions, footstools, table-cloths, d'oyleys, *couvre-pieds*, valances for chimney-pieces, and screens of all kinds. The unmeaning fret-work and commonplace silk lining of an upright piano may be replaced most agreeably by a piece of silk embroidery. This should be of fine and careful work, for it is fully displayed, near the eye, and almost occupies the place of a picture. Bell-pulls remain in old-fashioned houses, and are coming into use again with the Jacobean style now in favour; they have a good effect embroidered on some colour that goes well with the wall paper or paint of the wainscot.

Embroidery on linen has as many uses as that on cloth or silk. Embroidered linen makes pleasant summer chair-covers, hangings for a morning-room or bedroom, valances to hang above a washstand, and borders for brackets. Afternoon tea table-cloths of linen look very well with embroidered ends—towel-wise—or bordered all round: outline work is more suitable for these than filled-in embroidery, as it will bear more frequent washing, especially if done in ingrain cotton. The indispensable ever-to-be-renewed "tidy" may be made quite a work of art. The most convenient material for tidies is linen, embroidered in various colours, or in monochrome with crewel or with filosel. Blue linen decorated with white makes a good useful tidy.

Outline work on linen is also very suitable for bedroom hangings; indeed, in our opinion, outline work is, as a rule, the best style for curtains and such large pieces of work, whatever the material may be; though beautiful coloured and filled-in work has been made for such purposes, and may be made again. To this class of work belong mats for the coal-box, bath carpets of coarse flannel, summer carriage rugs of heavy linen, and the large squares of linen used to protect the carpet by open windows. A little bold and effective embroidery for borders will make these necessaries into pleasant decorations, only they must not be too laboured, or made too conspicuous.

We have not yet named a class of work that has been favoured in all ages of needlework; one which will tax the skill of the needlewoman and designer perhaps even more than curtains, viz., the bed-quilt or coverlet. A quilt means, properly speaking, something quilted, *i.e.*, wadded and sewn down: very beautiful grounds were made in this way, the quilting being sometimes the sole ornament of the coverlet, and at others serving as a ground on which various patterns were worked. In these days, and with a decorative end in view, such very elaborate work hardly repays the time spent on it; but we do recommend the coverlet as an excellent object for work and for design. Outline work in one colour is very suitable for this purpose, and a bold formal pattern looks very handsome. A more flowing and branching design, well enclosed in lines and borders, will look equally well: the worker's name or monogram and the date should always be added. Quilts are sometimes made with Bolton sheeting, used rather as a foundation than as a ground, being nearly covered with an applied pattern of leaves and flowers in cloth, with the stems worked in crewel; the vacant spaces being filled by a very simple diaper.

For outline work a strong linen makes the best ground, and we advise that the pattern be worked in filosel, as more durable than worsted, and also as pleasanter in the working. For this purpose, and for any large piece of monochrome work, it is necessary to have an abundant supply of filosel or worsted; what remains need not be wasted, but if there be too little, it is scarcely possible to get it really matched; the colour may appear to be the same, but it will have been dyed at different times, and washing, or even wear, will develop a difference, that spoils the whole work.

From what we have said, it will be seen that, although skilled workers often employ valuable materials, yet true art needlework need not be costly. It is only necessary to observe the rules of art as regards the design and the colouring, in order to make the most inexpensive materials into objects that shall be a perpetual delight.

We must, however, give a caution against a mistake that frequently brings good needlework into contempt. It is that of filling a room with perpetual patterns: carpet and walls are perhaps already ornamented with more or less striking designs, and if we embroider every article susceptible of this decoration with patterns—however lovely—we shall lose the essential quality of repose, fatigue the eye, and weary the mind.

CHAPTER VI.

ON CHURCH EMBROIDERY.

THERE are two more branches of needlework closely connected with our subject, but as each is a study in itself, and has been the subject of able and exhaustive treatises, a few words on their relations to Art are all that need be given to either.

These two are—(1) Church Embroidery, and (2) Lace.

The first has been much studied at all times, and of late years more carefully than the decorative needlework of which we have been speaking, and with ever-improving results. Many works of true art have been produced, many also that have fallen lamentably short of that standard.

The study of church needlework has one curious disadvantage. Being in a certain measure the expression of religious thought, the examples we have of it are governed by the ideas of the time which produced them; but a long and interesting period of church history, full of growth and rich in thought, remains without examples.

The history of secular needlework is continuous, each century having its own style, depending upon and growing out of that which preceded it; while for nearly three hundred years no needlework whatever was done for our churches. During the time that furnishes 'us with the best specimens of secular needlework, green baize, red cloth, or, at best, crimson velvet with gold tassels, were all that was permitted for ecclesiastical decoration; consequently the history of church embroidery stops short in the sixteenth century, and there is no further guide, good or bad.

A new style is beset with the same difficulties that attend the revival, or rather the renewed practice of Gothic architecture. One of these difficulties is that later Continental examples, while often showing great technical skill, have as often defied every rule of Art, or are the expression of doctrines and ideas which do not find favour in this country or belong to the Anglican Church. But, in spite of all that has been said, a new style of church architecture is growing up adapted to present needs, and with it a new style of needlework must find a place, if indeed it has not already done so; the humbler art possessing fewer difficulties and more elasticity than the greater one on which it is dependent.

The general rules that have been given for the design and colouring of decorative needlework for our homes will also apply to that which is intended for the glory of God in the beautifying of His house. This last has narrower limitations, stricter laws of fitness, bonds of symbolism, rules of colour, and traditions of style; but a student of art needlework will not find these stricter laws prevent church work from being beautiful and harmonious; indeed, they will be aids rather than hindrances, while the knowledge already acquired of general principles of colour and design will be a safeguard against placing vulgar, crude, or tasteless combinations where, in many eyes, they would be not only ugly but irreverent.

Church needlework differs only from secular art-work in its design, which is subject to the limitations spoken of above, and in its special application, which makes it the highest effort of needlework. If a faithful apprenticeship has been served to secular work, it is only needful to apply the same principles to suitable designs in order to fit the work for the highest purpose to which it can be devoted. Instead of merely reproducing ancient work, which is often too cramped and archaic to suit modern churches, it will be better to employ the increased skill of modern times in designing work that shall be new and original, and yet within the fitting limits and chastened reserve of ecclesiastical embroidery.

In designing this kind of work the foregoing rules will be found especially binding. There are double reasons why colours should be grave and rich rather than harsh or crude: unity of design and harmony of colour take a new and deeper meaning, honesty of workmanship becomes a duty, and a new reason for conventionalism is seen when we remember that we ourselves, when in God's house, lay aside an ordinary and natural demeanour.

It seems impertinent to criticise a branch of needlework that we do not intend to teach, but it may not be amiss to warn our readers against some of the mistakes that are most frequently committed. One of these is the abuse of symbolism, as when symbols are wrongly used or put in wrong places. The most holy signs and names are often seen placed where they will be leant against, knelt upon, or even stood upon; or emblems are seen in positions of the highest dignity which should properly occupy only secondary places.

A more common fault, the result of a more common ignorance, is to suppose that precious materials, excellent workmanship, and even good colouring will atone for the absence of a thoughtful and well-balanced design; this is to endeavour to build without a foundation.

The pieces of work hitherto described have been shown as examples; one which we have seen must now be held up as a warning. It was an "antependium," or pulpit frontal, the material of which was cream-white silk. The border was of pale pink roses, with their stems and leaves on a ground of olive green, well treated and well worked. In the centre was a red cross bordered with gold, in harmony with the border, well proportioned, and rightly telling as the principal point. This would have been very good had this been all, and had the white ground been left plain as a relief to the eye, or worked with a diaper to give it increased richness, but it was encumbered with a heavy scroll above the cross, shaded with a cold inharmonious grey, and inscribed with black letters that made the sharpest contrast in the whole work. Below the cross were a large fleur-de-lys and a highly conventionalised rose, both in gold-coloured silk, exquisitely worked, but quite out of place, overloading and confusing the design.

Good work may be done for churches by many who are uninstructed in the details of the richer kinds of work; but they should content themselves with the humbler rather than the more ambitious objects. Besides these last, which from the dignity of their position and the richness of their materials require special skill and undivided attention, there are many articles the decoration of which may be confided to less practised hands. Kneeling cushions and pede-mats have been partly rescued from the dominion of cross-stitch, and are frequently embroidered or made in applied work of excellent design and colour. More seldom, but occasionally, we have seen embroidered colossal hangings and door curtains, which are much more beautiful and valuable than any loom work, upholstery, or the stamped designs most commonly used for these purposes.

To all these articles the rules of design and colour given in our earlier chapters will easily be applied, often more easily than in work intended for house decoration, because of the broader and simpler surroundings and equally distributed light of a church; while the varied and constantly changing uses and aspects of an ordinary room multiply the difficulties of arranging forms and colours for its decoration.

CHAPTER VII.

ON SOME KINDS OF LACE.

ONE more branch of needlework has to be mentioned, viz., Lace. With lace made on the pillow we have nothing to do, it is not needlework, and its beauties are not of the same order; but point lace, properly so called, made with points or stitches, comes into the category of art needlework, from its beautiful and expressive designs so marvellously adapted to the materials and conditions of its workmanship, and from its matchless execution. For everything but personal use, and for some church purposes, these triumphs of needlework are too costly and elaborate; but there are several kinds of lace, or rather linen work, which, as being more adapted for general purposes and for their decorative value, deserve a place with coloured embroidery. We do not, however, intend to give anything like full or sufficient directions for doing these kinds of work, but merely to mention the different styles of lace-work which seem best suited for decoration, and to give a few hints as to the rules of art to be applied to them.

We begin with the bolder kind of tape-guipure, which is made of linen tape twisted and folded into a pattern, held together with bars, and then filled in and enriched with needlework. For this work the pattern should be such as may be formed by the flat folds of the tape, cut and joined on again when required. No attempt should be made to conceal that it is a tape by drawing it into shapes that it will not easily take, or by making it imitate lace made entirely with the needle or upon the pillow. The best material for this work is a real tape—that is, one in which the threads cross each other at right angles, and not a braid which has no warp, the threads in which are plaited together. The bars or "brides" should be firm, not too thin, and sufficient in number to hold the tape well in its place, allowing no loose curves or ill-secured angles. It is better to have too many than too few bars, and, whether with or without knots, they should be of firm overcast or button-hole work, not merely of twisted threads. The thread used for the bars and for filling some of the spaces should neither be too fine nor too tightly twisted, in which case it is wiry and intractable. Even if the soft thread should seem to make the work fluffy and confused at first, the first wash will clear it more than enough.

With regard both to this guipure work and to the other kinds of linen work on which we are going to speak, the rule laid down in the first chapter for all decorative work applies—however complete, it should be easy. Therefore, lace-work done for this purpose should not be a monument of patient industry, into which as much work as possible is put, nor a sampler of various stitches and curious devices, but a clear and facile carrying out of the original idea, easy to be comprehended, and producing a good effect at a moderate distance.

A beautiful kind of work, which is founded upon old lace, though we believe the manner of executing it to be quite modern, is done by drawing patterns on linen, overcasting or buttonholing the outlines, cutting away the ground, and enriching the pattern with bars, cords, and raised work.

This kind of work admits of great richness both of form and execution; the beautiful flowing patterns of Venetian, rose, raised, or bone point can be very well reproduced in it, preserving their beauties of form and proportion; but if our meaning has been hitherto made clear, it will be understood that these laces must not be merely imitated, but carefully studied and adapted to the intended purpose. It is true that this mode of working is particularly well adapted to the patterns of the above-named laces; but for this reproduction they must be considerably enlarged and their detail much simplified, giving only their broader characteristics. If this be neglected, the linen will be only a coarse and unsatisfactory imitation of the close-set stitches of the original, instead of an arrangement of pleasant contrasts between the plainness and evenness of the linen, the spaces and bars of the ground, and the raised work of the edges. The outlining of this work with gold thread has a very rich and beautiful effect, which is increased if the lining be of amber or golden-brown silk or satin.

Point-conté, lately called "guipure d'art," or, in homely phrase, darned netting, is another effective kind of white needlework. It is almost the only kind of old work which, in modern practice, has preserved some degree of beauty, in spite of the fancy-work shops and ladies' magazines. This may be ascribed to the unyielding nature of the netted groundwork, which compels a certain special treatment, and thus vigorous and beautiful designs have been produced, but through blind rather than intelligent obedience. In the desire for variety rather than for appropriateness, later designs have been spoiled by cutting away portions of the net in order to produce larger open spaces, destroying the unity of the diaper-like ground and making uncomfortable-looking holes. The ground should be netted with linen thread, beginning at one corner; great care is needed to make it true and even, so that it will stretch properly in the little frames used for the work. The pattern should be worked in the same thread as that used for the ground. This is a very old kind of work; the early specimens are simply darned on the netting, without any raised work, in bold conventional designs, sometimes with letters, armorial bearings, and such devices.

Punto a gruppo, *point-tiré*, or drawn work, is a kind of linen work that is particularly good for decorative purposes; it is simple and easy, and produces an excellent effect. It is most appropriate for the ends of table-cloths, toilet-cloths, tidies, or towels: the last being its original Italian use. As the names indicate, it is made in the material of the cloth itself, some of the threads of which are drawn out and the remainder grouped into patterns more or less elaborate. A hem-stitch like that used for pocket handkerchiefs is useful for this work; it may be worked singly along a row of drawn threads, or, for a broader line, on both sides of the row, either taking up the same threads as those taken on the other side, so making little bars; or taking half the threads from each of two of the opposite stitches, and so making a zig-zag. Other patterns may be made by passing a thick linen thread along the centre of a row of threads from which the weft has been drawn, and either twisting them over each other or knotting them into groups. (See Plate VII.)

Pretty work may be made by embroidering the spaces of plain

linen between the rows of drawn work, either with silk or with ingrain cotton, red or blue; only one colour should be used; the cotton should be the thickest that can be procured, and a little of it or of the silk should be mixed with the fringe. The patterns worked should be very simple, either line patterns, dots, stars, or very simple leaf patterns. Our own taste is in favour of using only one kind of work, rather than a mixture of drawn work and embroidery; but the latter is so much admired that we give these few hints for it, with the advice that in mixed work one or the other kind should be made the most prominent. If the prominence is intended to be given to the embroidery, the drawn work should be distinctly subservient; but if the contrary, the embroidery should be confined to narrow patterns of the simplest kind. This work washes extremely well, and so does the cotton or silk embroidery; it should not be starched or ironed, but pinned or basted flat and tight while wet upon a board or the floor, and left to dry.

Drawn work should be finished with a fringe of the warp of the material knotted or twisted into tassels. The elaboration of this knotted fringe gave rise to what is now known as *Macrame* lace, a kind of work that has often a very good effect. The old specimens are very beautiful; but the modern revival is not always happy, partly because the thread used is too smooth and tightly twisted, making the work too regular and machine-like; partly because the patterns are too elaborate, and the threads are too much tied, instead of being left partly loose and showing their real nature; and the easy, natural look, which is the great charm of the work, is thus lost. By avoiding these faults, and remembering the character of the work as a finish and fringe rather than a lace, very good edges and borders may be made.

Perhaps the most beautiful work and the best art production of all these laces is *point-coupé*, or cut work, erroneously called Greek lace. It is made on a foundation of linen, of which some of the threads are cut away and the remainder worked over, making regular square spaces. A severe ground plan, as it may be called, is thus laid down, and the pattern, however rich and varied, is subdued and confined by guiding lines, and may be made to form stars, circles, crosses, or cobwebs of a geometrical character. As the limits imposed by the manner of working cannot be passed, this work is never seen in a bad style, even when the severe right angles of the foundation are partly overcome, and the scollops and vandykes that were once only the edge of the straight border are enlarged and developed until they form the principal part of the work; the geometric character is preserved, and the work, which by its first conditions restrains while it exercises the fancy and skill of the worker, is still beautiful and excellent.

Cut work is very durable, and old examples of it are numerous; it was a great favourite with the painters of the 17th century, and is found in every portrait, forming the turned-up cuffs of the Vandyke dress, and edging the falling collars that displaced the standing ruffs of the previous half-century. The finer kinds of this work are very laborious, though labour is seldom better spent; for furniture decoration it can hardly be too coarse, provided the material be sufficiently durable to repay the trouble of the working. Brown packing cloth for the foundation—which is entirely covered —worked with brown thread, in a suitable pattern, with not more detail than the thick threads can express clearly, will make a beautiful border. This may be edged with a *Macrame* fringe of the same thread as is used for the work, care being taken that the knotted pattern be quite simple and unobtrusive, so as not to divide attention with the border, to which it is only an adjunct.

For the borders at the ends of a white linen altar-cloth, this lace should be worked on stout white linen with a thick soft white linen thread; this admits of a very rich pattern, and is admirably suited to the purpose. The lace should be firmly finished off with a flat hem of the foundation linen all round, making it complete in itself. A fringe of linen thread should be sewn on, so that it can be renewed. The cloth, of finer linen, should have a broad open hem all round; if crosses are added, they should be worked in thick embroidery with fine linen thread. Then the cloth should be washed twice over, and got up without starch. Last of all, the cut-work borders should be sewn to the ends of the cloth with an open stitch, which may be easily cut when the cloth is washed, which it will require much more frequently than the borders.

For the histories, dates, and other particulars of these laces, the reader is referred to the works of Mrs. Bury-Palliser and Mrs. Hailstone, which contain not only every information to be desired, but also illustrations from which patterns can be worked or adapted.

The materials for each kind of work mentioned in this chapter are the same, *i.e.*, linen cloth and linen thread of various degrees of whiteness and fineness, the choice and matching of which require some considerable skill and judgment, only to be gained by experience. One hint only we can give, and that must not be taken for an invariable rule—viz., patent and specially-made materials should be avoided. Work is almost certain to be truer, easier, and more full of character if made of ordinary household materials, than of articles made purposely for the "fancy trade." Homespun linen and thread are, unfortunately for our purposes, hardly to be met with now, and machine-made fabrics are only too even and white; but a better choice can be made at the linen-draper's than at the fancy shop, if care is always taken that, whether fine or coarse, each article be true and good of its kind.

CHAPTER VIII.

ON THE STUDY OF OLD NEEDLEWORK.

THE interesting subject of the history of ancient needlework is far too wide to be entered upon here, but as acquaintance with good models is essential to the successful practice of this as of every other art, we will give a few hints on what is best to study or to imitate.

We would not by any means be understood to insist that because work is old it is necessarily beautiful. Its beauty, like that of modern work, will depend on its obedience to the laws of art, though much of its peculiar charm lies in this obedience being unconscious; the workwoman or designer could have laid down no rules for expressing a sense of beauty and proportion, but she has succeeded nevertheless, perhaps rather the more, in putting them into her work. Partly, no doubt, the work, if it be good, gains its charm with age; the colours soften and mellow; the linen takes a creamy tint; the stitches fit into their places in the loving companionship of years; and the mystery of past generations—of the busy fingers quiet now, of hopes faded or fulfilled, of stories that must be ever untold—hangs about the fragments that we tenderly handle and carefully preserve.

Much of the old needlework that has been handed down to

us is not suitable for our imitation, though almost all is worthy of study. Tapestry, for instance, may give many useful hints. When the work is of sufficiently early date to be pure in style, the flowers and stems of flowering plants are often very good, well conventionalised and yet full of life. Flower-stems dividing the figure subjects of old work are often particularly good, and are worthy of notice in pictures, and in wood or stone carving, as well as in needlework. But tapestry is not suitable for our imitation; it is too elaborate in the later specimens, and too archaic in the early ones; with our skill, knowledge, and appliances we can do more, and to better purpose, for decorative effect in other ways.

Better models may be found in the freer work of the 17th and 18th centuries, and in the early part of the present century. All embroidery on linen grounds, whether in silks or worsteds, is well worthy of attention. In this style are massive quilts of the 17th century, with bold flower patterns overlaying an elaborately quilted ground, all done in silk, sometimes many coloured, and sometimes in the beautiful pale gold colour of undyed silk. There is also coarser work of the same century in crewel worsteds; some of these are very handsome and well designed, while others are clumsy in design and gaudy in colour. Samplers are more to be considered for their curious and quaint devices than as possessing beauties worthy of imitation. It is sometimes well to remark their extreme conventionalism, and a hint may thus be gleaned for use in larger work.

The curtains and hangings of Queen Anne's time are of excellent design, grave and well-considered. Here is no more quaintness, no striving after the impossible, nor touching imperfection, rousing our sympathy for the eager and fanciful workwoman of the earlier time.

All is polished, capable, well-regulated, the colour entirely within bounds, the forms full of a courtly rather than a natural grace. The flowers are not those of the forest and wild hedgerow, but of grave parterres and stately Dutch gardens—noble sunflowers curling their leaves within due bounds, tulips standing upright on sufficient stems, stiff crown imperials and broad lilies, all marshalled in well-balanced order and thoughtful arrangement. For large pieces of work, such as coverlets and curtains, there cannot be better models than these, always having regard to the intended surroundings of our own work.

Lighter and more delicate fancies succeed these stately performances; the patterns grow smaller, the materials finer, the uses more intimate and personal. Trailing patterns of honeysuckle, jasmine, and sweet pea cover the finer linen in graceful trellis, or are scattered over creamy satin in dainty bouquets and sprigs, of which the best chintz patterns are imitations. Delicate satin-stitch work is done on net—almost worthy of being ranked as lace; and embroidery on white muslin is brought to a rare perfection. Silk is dyed in more tender shades; velvet becomes too heavy for the prevailing taste, and goes much out of fashion; crewels are less used, and silks more so; while the linen becomes cambric, and satin —the most beautiful material of all—is most frequently used for a ground.

We can hardly study the needlework of the 18th century too much; but it must be as intelligent students, not as servile copyists —not accepting as good everything of that date, for it is beauty, not curious antiquity, that we seek. It is because the work of this time is thoughtful and original that it is worthy of our earnest attention; but in blind admiration we are apt to miss these essential charms. It is well to remember the reason why English art-work of this period is so good: it is because there was then so little pacific intercourse with the French, from whom we have always been too prone to copy; our workmen were thrown upon their own resources, and, consequently, there is in all the household and decorative work of this age something more truly national and more original than at any subsequent period.

Speaking of a living artist, Professor Sidney Colvin says:— "For surroundings, for motive, for costume, he has been apt to turn towards the England of the 18th century—as who would not turn of such as care for simple refinement and reserve in outward things, for a natural and demure inventiveness in the accessories of life that is full of an inexpressible charm? This is not the place for an apology of that century, which its successor has from many sides flouted and disowned with such blatant and ignorant ingratitude; besides, the instinct of artists has in our day led more than one of them to do their part towards its rehabilitation, at least on the side of its home look and garniture, and the lovable circumstances with which it invested its ladyhood and childhood—exquisite these, if ever they were exquisite on earth."* Nowhere shall we find this delicate feeling, these lovable circumstances, more clearly and truly expressed than in the needlework these ladies loved.

Continental work must be studied in the same way as our own. The churches and museums of numberless foreign towns contain pieces of needlework easily accessible and well worthy of attention. As an instance, there are several interesting fragments in the Imperial Museum at Nuremberg; one, the "Battle of the Frogs," a spirited

* "Portfolio," May, 1871.

work in white thread on blue linen, is from Portugal, and suggests yet unknown treasures in that country. Italy is, in this as in other arts, the great storehouse of examples; the rich domestic life of the free cities has produced the best specimens that remain to us of the labours of former centuries in this peculiarly domestic art. In Italy, the best and brightest silk for the needle, as well as the finest textile fabrics, were produced; but it is not so much the excellence of the materials as the art knowledge and feeling it exhibits that make Italian needlework so beautiful. But though this may be the best, the productions of every country should be considered, and there are few that do not produce something which may be instructive. Attention should always be paid to patterns that appear to be traditional, and used for the same purposes from generation to generation. An instance of this is the highly-conventionalised and very effective pot-and-flower pattern that the Cretan women embroider in silk on their linen petticoats.

Oriental needlework has, until the last few years, been produced under the same conditions as old English work; that is, the styles are of natural growth, and the work has been done for home uses and under national influences—not to satisfy foreign tastes or to supply a foreign market.

Indian, Chinese, and Japanese needlework is better for study than for close imitation. The first is often very beautiful in the colouring—no western race seems to have understood polychrome so well; we include Persian and Cashmere work, with the varied products of Hindoo looms and needles, all that is kindred and yet dissimilar coming under the term "Indian," taken in its widest sense. To study this colouring with profit, we must only take work done before the introduction of modern European dyes;

good patterns are now too often totally spoiled by the use of English aniline-dyed silks; and there are others, for the most part good, where pieces of magenta-pink stand out like painful blots, while older pieces in the same style are models of bright harmonious colouring. Indian needlework done in gold and silver is especially beautiful, and looks splendid without being gaudy. We shall do well to notice that, when gold is used with varied colours, it is as precious and well-applied as in the best 14th century illuminations.

The beauties of Japanese needlework are, like those of other art-work from that wonderful land, very far from being rightly understood here by more than a few; and though a wave of fashion has swept numberless objects of Japanese art into this country, their real merits are as yet but little appreciated. It must be remembered that Japanese work, like our own, to be good, must conform to the rules of art; and also that, without knowing the nature of the objects represented, we are apt to call objects strange and barbarous which are often conventionalisms and symbols, meaningless to us simply because we do not possess the key. Here the caution against rash copying needs repetition. It is in great measure to unintelligent imitation of the Japanese that we owe some of the extraordinary productions of the last few years. These show only one, and that one of the least important, of the characteristics of good art—originality, and the only emotion they excite in the beholder is the not very elevated one of amazement.

The best specimens of Japanese needlework are the cloths used as covers for the presents given by persons paying visits of ceremony; these cloths are not given with the presents they cover, but are family heirlooms, and good specimens are rarely seen in

England. The white birds on a black satin ground, so often met with, are done for the English market; they have many merits, but are far inferior to the work done by the Japanese for their own honour and delight. Some rare pieces we have seen lately were excellent illustrations of the principles of colour recommended in Chapter III.; the grounds are satin, of the deep soft blue of a summer night, and the leading colours of the embroidery are gold, pale blue, and white. Another piece we will describe in detail, as it gives a good idea of Japanese excellences of design and arrangement. The ground is scarlet moreen; of a bright scarlet, yellow enough to harmonise with the gold that forms the principal colour in the embroidery. The subject is a long flight of storks, the sacred bird—not less than eighty of them are flying upwards in a zigzag line, the angles of which are very carefully studied, from the bottom to the top of the picture. Most of these storks are in white silk, the direction of the stitches giving much of their form; they are picked out with black, and there is a little pale pink or pale yellow-green in their beaks and legs. A few of them, perhaps one-fourth, are worked all in gold, representing the birds in shadow, or seen against the light, and these have little or no detail. Each bird is distinct, separately drawn, and having his own expression, mode of flight, and position in the line. The rest of the space is filled by horizontal bars of gold of varying widths, and groups of fan-stitches also in gold; these seem to indicate the flat sunset clouds, and the tops of the distant trees passed over by the storks in their flight.

We have specially described this piece of needlework because it so truly conforms to the rules of the art, and exhibits the greatest richness, delicacy, and elaboration within the strict limits of needlework. There is no shading, but the forms of the storks are accurately expressed by the direction of the stitches as well as by the colour. The detail is abundant where the storks are in light, and is expressed by the varied and manageable silks. The truth that colour and detail are lost when objects are seen against the light is recognised in the treatment of the golden storks, which are in flat shapes of plain gold. Any attempt to give the varied colours and shapes of the clouds would have interfered with the effect of the storks, which are the motive of the whole, so their horizontal character and varying widths are the truths chosen for representation. So with the trees: a few fan-stitches just express their multitude, their rounded lines against the sky, and the way in which each tree springs from its own centre; other details, such as colour, shadow, variety, roundness, &c., are beyond the limits of the needlework, and are wisely let alone.

In studying patterns and arrangements of colour for the sake of our needlework, we must not by any means confine ourselves to needlework only; the productions of other arts will often be found useful, especially Oriental arts. Most Eastern needlework is too elaborate for imitation; but when it is fully understood what is and what is not suitable for our own work, many hints may be gathered, and even whole patterns successfully adapted from carved or inlaid work, from enamels, metal-work, or from china. For instance, the flower-drawing on Japanese hand-screens and fans is an excellent study; the flowers are simple, clear, and vividly expressed in themselves, and also admirably adapted to the size and shapes of the spaces they ornament. Good line patterns are often to be found on the insides of china cups and basins. Indian weapons, ornamented with damascened work, will give hints for conventional patterns in outline. Moorish metal-work has often good incised line patterns, and so forth. In European art there is not so much to be easily adapted to our purposes; but in early Italian, Flemish, and German pictures—in wood-carving in low relief, in incised metal-work, and other similar things, there is nearly always something to be learned, provided that the objects we study are good of their kind, and true to their own art.

Returning to the needlework of our own country, it seems that, from the time that Indian and Chinese fabrics were brought here, English taste has decayed; the skill and patience of Eastern workers seem to have stricken English ones with despair. Odd imitations of Indian and Chinese pattern and colouring are found in some manufactures—such as Lowestoft and old Worcester ware, and Manchester printed cottons—falling far short of the models, it is true, but showing a growing appreciation of their beauty. This, together with the effect of renewed French influence, helped to bring on the strange era in which everything was an imitation, and nothing was original, natural, or spontaneous of its own kind; when the work of bygone centuries was ticketed and copied without intelligence or taste—not enquired into, studied, or comprehended; a time in which every art was paralysed—in which old things were not understood, and new things were mere imitations, barren and lifeless.

Into the causes of this deadness and debasement we cannot here enquire; it was probably not so much a deadness as a winter sleep before a new spring; it is sufficient for the present purpose to believe it to be over, and, laying a good foundation of what is old, to build up that which is new, work not less true than the old, but more spacious, wide and firm, above all, more beautiful; having always regard to the eternal laws that, by truth and fitness, govern beauty.

We cannot expect our work to have the natural unconscious grace of early art that was the spontaneous production of the taste and skill of its time, and in which there was little intentional reference to what had gone before or to what might be hereafter. Every condition of art has undergone change; the past is laid before us as an open book, and we cannot choose but read in it; the styles of bygone centuries are known, named, and enquired into, and are open to every student.

Surrounded by so many guides and models, it may well be feared that any new excellence is impossible for us; but, avoiding on the one hand the imitation of that which is imperfect and inappropriate, and on the other the struggle after originality that ends in eccentricity, and availing ourselves of the knowledge, skill, enlightenment, and improved appliances of the age, we may yet produce good and tasteful work, not quite unworthy of the high rank we claim for it in using the name Art Needlework.

CHAPTER IX.

THE PLATES.

WITH regard to the designs which form so important a part of this work, it is necessary to state—as it has been found impossible to produce them in their full size and still to preserve a portable form—that while some are drawn on a sufficiently large scale for working, others will have to be enlarged, some more and some less, according to the nature of the piece of work intended and the space to be filled. As any attempt to represent stitches or texture would have had but an unsatisfactory result, the designs are printed in flat tints merely, and it will be found that any undue flatness and hardness will disappear in the execution; and the designs, if properly carried out in needlework, will appear to far greater advantage than they now do in colour-printing. In some of the designs for filled-in work, a thin outline has been found necessary in order to define the forms, but this is not intended to be reproduced in needlework.

PLATE I.—Design for square footstool or cushion—strawberry blossom and leaves. If used for a footstool, it should be worked in crewels on cloth or serge; if for a cushion, in silks on silk or satin; or it may be worked on woollen stuff partly in crewels and partly in silk. It will be seen that this design is adapted to its purpose by looking equally well in any position, it being impossible to be placed upside down. It may be enlarged to any size required for either of the above-named purposes. Half-a-yard square is a good size for a cushion. The border at the foot of the plate is intended for the sides of the footstool, and would not be required for the cushion.

PLATE II.—Contains two designs; the upper one is intended for the border of a table-cloth—primroses, wood-anemones, and ivy—to be worked in crewels on cloth or serge; the flowers may be worked in silk. The design may be enlarged, if required. The lower design is for a mantelpiece border—oranges and blossom—which may be enlarged and continued to fit the required size, the basket to come in the centre; to be worked on cloth, serge, or velvet, in silk or crewel according to taste. The former of these two designs illustrates a somewhat naturalistic treatment, while the latter is more formal and decorative.

PLATE III.—Design for curtains, to be worked in two shades of blue, in crewels on linen or Bolton sheeting. This design may be worked in its present scale, or it may be enlarged if desired.

PLATE IV.—Design for tidy or chair-back—chrysanthemum—to be worked on linen in crewels and silk. It should be enlarged to three or four times its present size.

PLATE V.—The same design as that in Plate IV., but in different colouring.

THE PLATES.

PLATE VI.—Design for a cushion—syringa—to be worked on cloth or velvet in silk or crewels. The border, which is shown at the top of the plate, is intended to be repeated at each of the four sides; and the small square, shown at the foot of the plate, to be repeated at each of the four corners. The design may be enlarged to any extent not exceeding four times its present size.

PLATE VII.—Patterns of stitches for table-cloth, toilet-cloth, tidy, or towels, with fringe at the foot—produced in any loosely-woven material by drawing out warp or woof threads in definite places, and twisting, looping, gathering up, or knotting the loose threads that are left.

PLATE VIII.—Contains two designs: (1) Border for table-cover—wild clematis, or traveller's joy—to be worked on cloth or serge; the flowers in silk, and the rest in crewels. Full size. (2) Design for a pocket or *gibecière*—speedwell—to be worked in silks on velvet.

PLATE IX.—Design for quilt, tidy, or chair-back. To be worked in crewels on glass-cloth, in which the squares are already defined and woven in colour, but the lines should be worked over.

PLATE X.—Design for curtain—honeysuckle and bird (yellow-hammer)—to be worked in crewels on linen, Bolton sheeting, or serge, which latter may be of a full colour if desired, so that it is harmonious. The bird should only be repeated half as often as the rest of the pattern, which need not be enlarged, but may be so if required.

PLATE XIV.—Design for tea-table cloth. Silk, on linen. Pale blue or pink may be used instead of yellow, if preferred.

PLATE XV.—Design for piano decoration—the space in a cottage or cabinet piano usually filled by silk and fret-work—to be worked in silks on silk, satin, or velvet. One-half of the design only is given, which will have to be enlarged to the required size, and repeated, reversed, for the other half.

PLATE XVI.—Design, chiefly outline, for curtains or *portière*, to be worked in silk or crewel on serge or cloth. It may be enlarged to any size, and the colour varied if required.

PLATE XVII.—Design for bed-hanging, curtain, or quilt, with border, which, in a quilt, should be worked all round. Silk, on unbleached linen or sheeting. Blue or red may be used instead of yellow, if preferred.

PLATE XVIII.—The same design reversed, white on colour. This design may be enlarged to any size.

PLATE XIX.—Border—periwinkle—which may be worked in silk or crewels, for a cloth table-cover, or for the border of a curtain or *portière*.

PLATE XI.—Outline design for tea-table cloth, to be worked in silk on linen; yellow, pink, or any other colour of a delicate shade may be used. The design does not require enlarging.

THE PLATES.

PLATE XII.—The same design reversed—light upon dark ground.

PLATE XIII.—Design for footstool—daisies—to be worked in crewels on serge or cloth; the border is intended to go round the side of the stool, and to be connected with the top by a cord or piping. To be enlarged to two or three times its present size.

1

11

111

IV

V

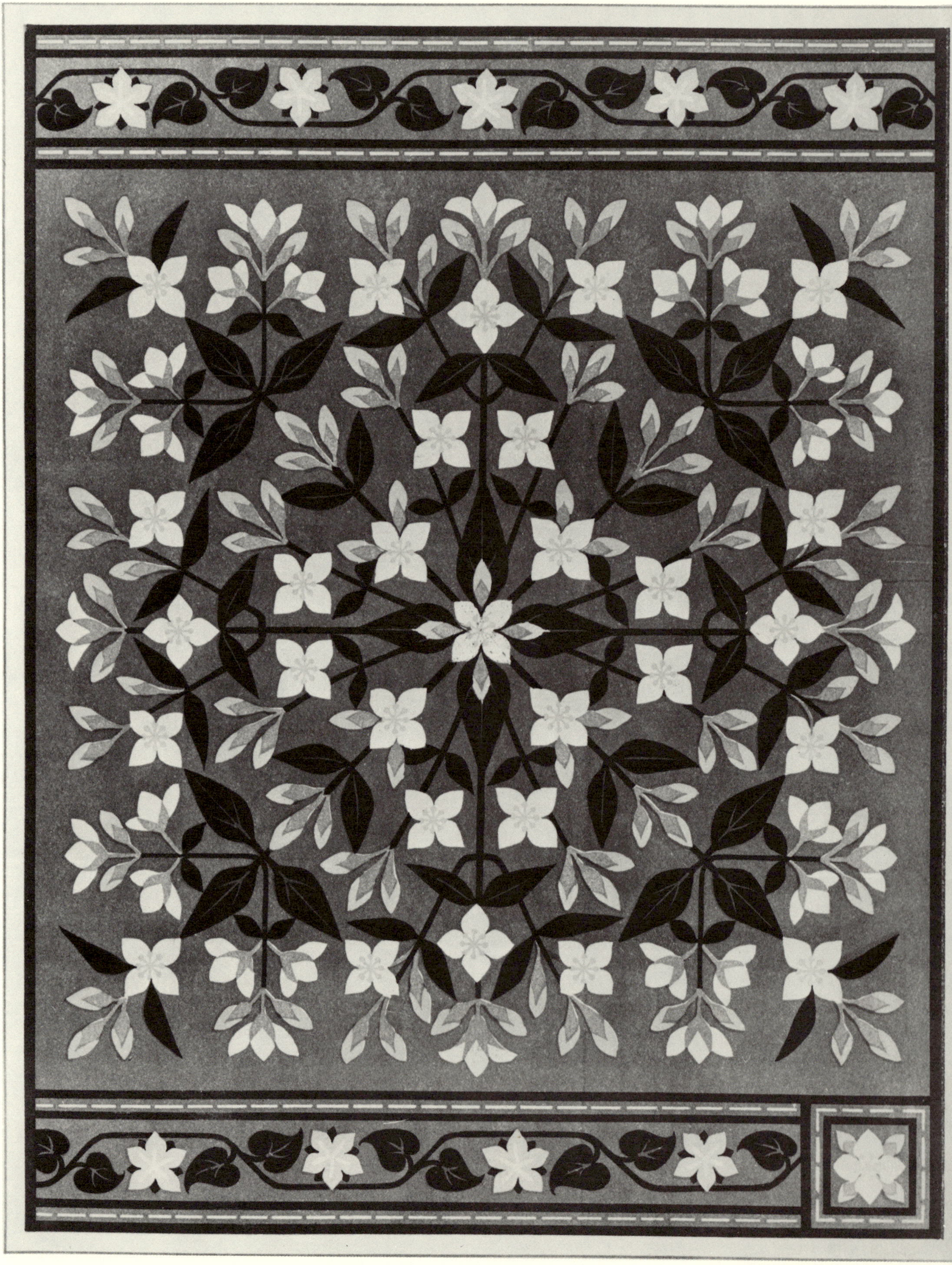

VII

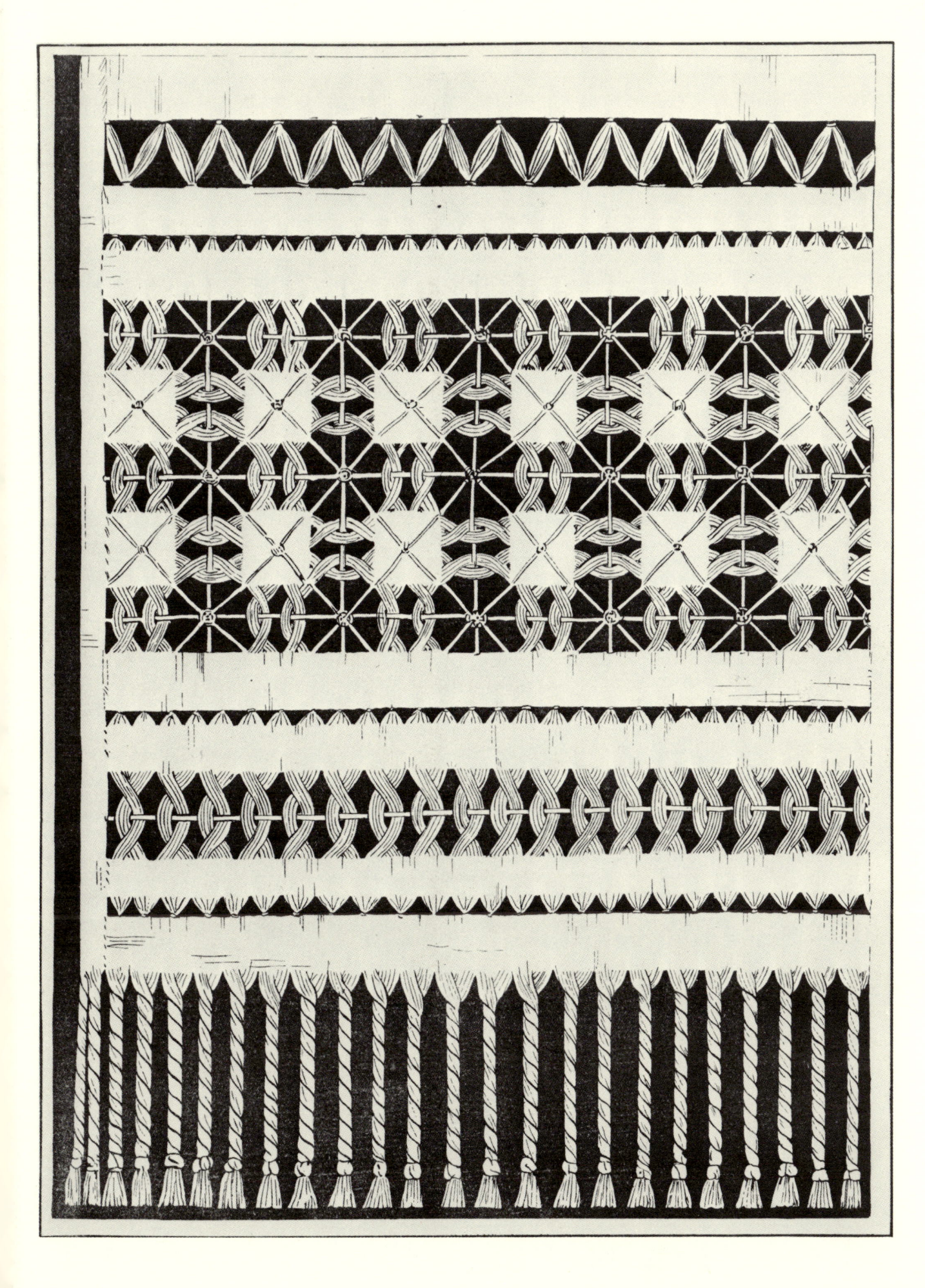

VIII

VIII

IX

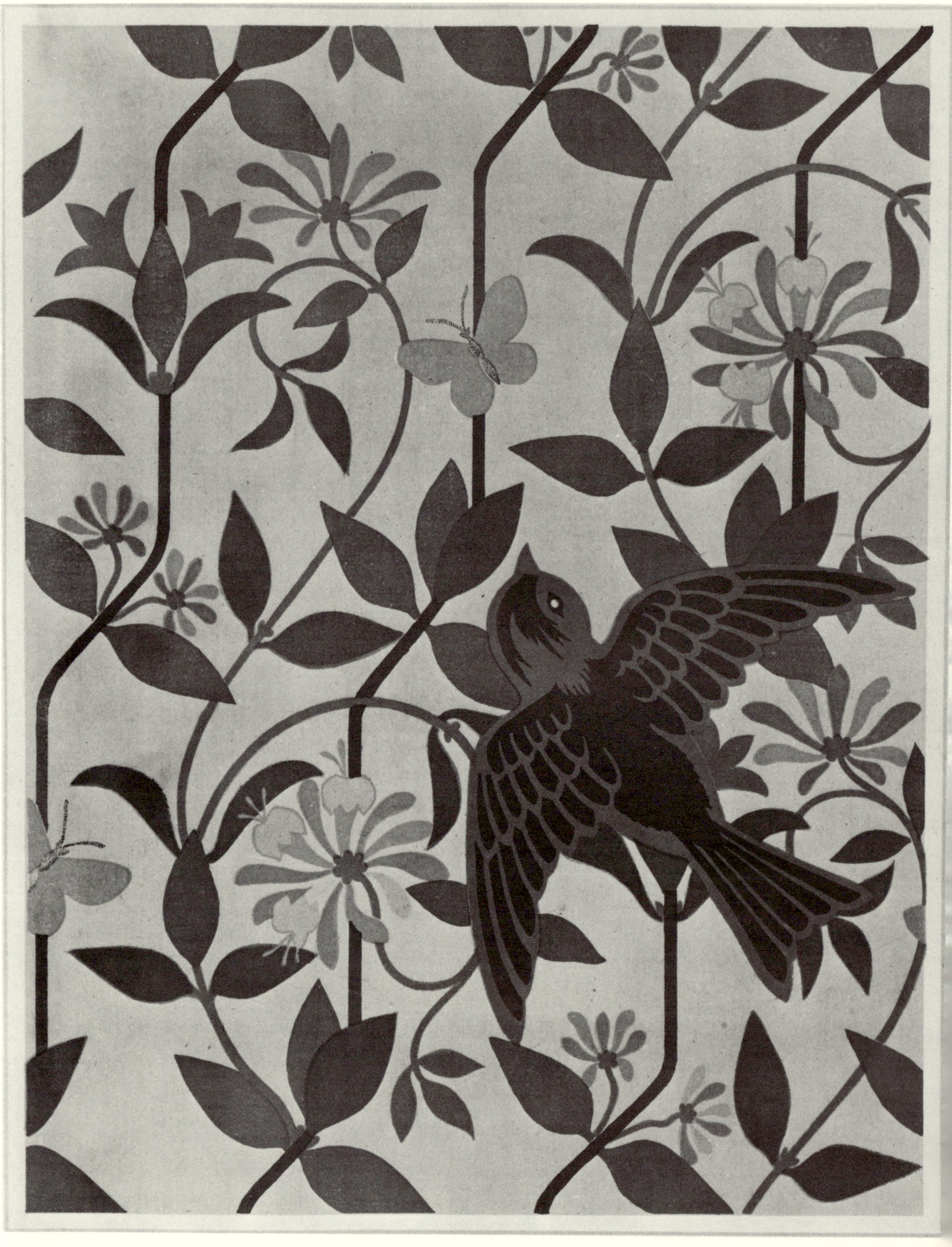

XI

X

XIII

XI

XV

XV

XVI

XV

XVIII

XI